D1203576

PARANORMAL FILES
ALIEN ENCOUNTERS

Stuart Webb

ROSEN
PUBLISHING®
New York

This edition published in 2013 by:

The Rosen Publishing Group, Inc.
29 East 21st Street, New York, NY 10010

Editor and Picture Researcher: Joe Harris
U.S. Editor: Andrea Sclarow
Design: Jane Hawkins
Cover Design: Jane Hawkins

Library of Congress Cataloging-in-Publication Data

Webb, Stuart.
Alien encounters/Stuart Webb.—1st ed.
    p. cm.—(Paranormal files)
Includes bibliographical references and index.
ISBN 978-1-4488-7172-8 (library binding)
1. Human-alien encounters. I. Title.
BF2050.W43 2012
001.942--dc23

2011052089

Manufactured in China

SL001881US

Picture Credits:
Cover: inset (left): Shutterstock. Inset (right): Corbis.
Interior pages: B. Barber: 1, 3, 10, 14, 20, 23, 32, 45, 46, 50, 60, 65, 66, 69. Clip Art: 9. Corbis: 16, 37, 39, 40, 43, 55. Getty: 59. Mary Evans: 26, 29, 31, 33, 52, 53, 56, 62, 71, 73t, 73b, 74. P. Gray: 5, 17, 48. Shutterstock:
1, 3, 10, 14, 20, 23, 32, 45, 46, 50, 60, 65, 66, 69. T. Boyer: 19, 25, 35, 78.

CPSIA Compliance Information: Batch #S12YA: For Further Information contact Rosen Publishing, New York, New York at 1-800-237-9932

CONTENTS

The Aliens Emerge...4

Alien Encounters 18

Alien Contact 42

Alien Abductions... 60

Glossary 76

Further Information 78

Index.. 79

THE ALIENS EMERGE

During the late 1940s and 1950s, many people around the world, especially in the US, began reporting sightings of UFOs. Speculation grew about what the objects were. Some thought that they might be secret weapons being tested by the military of the US or Soviet Union. Others thought they might be natural phenomena of some kind. Increasingly popular was the idea that the UFOs were alien spacecraft. This notion began to gain support when eyewitness reports emerged alleging that UFOs were solid, mechanical objects, crewed by intelligent beings that were definitely not human.

The Botta Encounter

In 1950, former pilot Dr. Enrique Botta was working as an engineer on a construction project in rural Bahia Blanca, some 75 miles (120 km) from Caracas, Venezuela. According to Botta, he was driving back to his hotel one evening when he saw a strange object resting in a field. He stopped the car to take a better look. The object, as he described it, was shaped like a domed disk made of a silvery metal. It had no legs or landing gear and seemed to be resting slightly askew. There was an open door on one side.

Botta got out of his car, walked across the field toward the object and peered through the door. Inside he could see a small, empty room lit by a hazy glow and a flashing red light. As Botta touched the object he noticed that although it looked as if it were made of metal, the skin of the craft had a jelly-like softness. Walking inside, Botta passed into a second, much larger room.

In that room Botta saw a curved bench or sofa on which sat three figures facing away from him. Each figure was about 4 ft (1.2 m) tall and dressed in a tight-fitting garment that reached to the neck. The heads were rather large and looked bald.

Botta stopped in alarm, but when the figures took no notice of him he approached them. As he got close he saw that the three figures were facing what he assumed to be a control panel. It was filled with gauges, lights and

car and drove to the hotel where he and his fellow engineers were staying.

Botta blurted out his story to his two closest colleagues. One of them had a gun he used for hunting. He suggested that the three of them return to the craft to inspect it further. It was by now dark, so the men decided to go in the morning.

Dr. Enrique Botta's description of bald aliens with domed heads is highly typical of eyewitness descriptions of aliens.

what seemed to be meters. Above the panel floated a transparent sphere that rotated slowly.

As the figures still took no notice of him, Botta reached out and touched one. The humanoid was rigid and hard, and its skin had the texture of charred wood. Believing that the beings were dead, Botta fled. He dashed back to his

Alien Files

DO PEOPLE REALLY HAVE ALIEN ENCOUNTERS?

Most of the encounters described in this book were witnessed by one or two people, or a small group at most. There is usually little or no physical evidence of the encounter to support their stories. So we are forced to rely almost exclusively on the eyewitness reports themselves. We must ask ourselves how reliable the witnesses are. It is possible that the encounter was the product of a lucid (real-seeming) dream or hallucination, or false-memory syndrome. False memories are sometimes created in the course of psychotherapy. Some stories might even be deliberate hoaxes. However, the possibility always remains that the witnesses *did* have an extraterrestrial encounter. Scientists will probably never be able to prove that UFOs and aliens don't exist.

The next morning, the three men drove back to the site of the encounter, but the disk-shaped craft had gone. According to them, all that was left was a small pile of ashes. One of Botta's friends stooped to touch it. It was hot and his hand allegedly turned purple, so he dropped the ash. They later claimed they spotted a UFO circling high overhead. It was shaped like a cigar and pulsed with a red glow. After a few minutes it flew off and the men were left alone.

Later that day Botta apparently collapsed with a fever and was rushed to the hospital. His skin broke out in a rash and began to blister. A test showed no sign of radiation, and the doctors thought that a very severe case of sunburn was the most likely explanation, although Botta had not been out in the sun much due to his job. Botta recovered after a few days and returned to work. He decided not to talk about the incident, but later as news of UFO sightings became more common in South America, he elected to speak out.

The Squyres Encounter

As intriguing as the Botta encounter was, it gave no clue about who the "ufonauts" were, where they came from or why they were visiting. What UFO researchers (ufologists) were hoping for was an encounter with a living alien – known as a close

encounter of the third kind (or CE3).

Perhaps the first report of a close encounter of the third kind to receive public attention occurred on August 25, 1952. William Squyres, a radio worker in Pittsburg, Kansas, was driving to work through farmland at 5:30 am along Highway 60. As he drove he apparently saw something odd in a pasture field. The following story is based on his description of what happened next.

As he drew closer he saw the object was silvery-gray in color, about 70 ft (21 m) across and 12 ft (3.7 m) high. It was shaped, Squyres said, rather like two soup bowls placed rim to rim and then flattened somewhat.

Squyres drove up until he was alongside the field and only about 300 ft (90 m) from the object. He then stopped his car and studied the object more closely. He could now see that the underside had a faint bluish glow to it. Around the object's edge was a rim or walkway. From this rose a number of vertical poles, each topped by what seemed to be a spinning propeller. The object was making a dull, throbbing noise.

At one end of the object there were what seemed to be slightly opaque windows through which indistinct objects could be seen moving. At the other end was a completely clear window through which a man could be seen apparently fiddling with controls or instruments. As far as Squyres could make out, the man was definitely human.

Fascinated, Squyres got out of his car to get a better look. Instantly the object began to rise vertically, the throbbing noise increasing in volume as it did so. The object continued to rise slowly for some seconds, then suddenly accelerated and flew off at high speed.

Enrique Botta claims that on entering a grounded UFO, he found three crew members apparently dead and slumped over a control panel.

Squyres reported the incident to the US Air Force (USAF) in case he had seen some sort of advanced foreign aircraft. An air force officer arrived a couple of days later and asked to be shown the site. He reported that he found, in the center of the field, the long grass had been squashed flat in a circle about 60 ft (18 m) in diameter. The grass stems had all been bent over, but not broken, and they formed a swirling spiral pattern. The officer collected samples of grass and soil and sent them off for analysis – which later found nothing at all unusual.

This sighting shows many features of what UFO researchers call a "close encounter of the second kind" (also called a CE2). In this kind of encounter, a sighting of a UFO is combined with evidence of its impact on its surroundings. However because Squyres said he also saw a pilot, UFO researchers would classify the sighting as a close encounter of a third kind.

Mary Starr's Experience

On December 16, 1957, Mrs. Mary Starr, a retired teacher living in Old-Saybrook, Connecticut, said she was awoken at about 2 am by a bright light shining into her bedroom. She looked out of the window to see a cigar-shaped object hovering about 15 ft (4.5 m) away in her backyard.

According to Starr, the object was about 30 ft (9 m) long and dark gray in color. Along the side was a series of

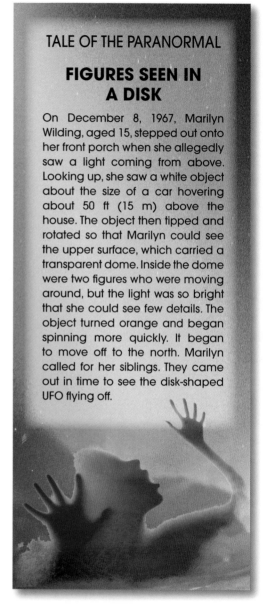

TALE OF THE PARANORMAL

FIGURES SEEN IN A DISK

On December 8, 1967, Marilyn Wilding, aged 15, stepped out onto her front porch when she allegedly saw a light coming from above. Looking up, she saw a white object about the size of a car hovering about 50 ft (15 m) above the house. The object then tipped and rotated so that Marilyn could see the upper surface, which carried a transparent dome. Inside the dome were two figures who were moving around, but the light was so bright that she could see few details. The object turned orange and began spinning more quickly. It began to move off to the north. Marilyn called for her siblings. They came out in time to see the disk-shaped UFO flying off.

square windows from which a bright light streamed. Through the windows, Starr could see two men walking around. The object was only about 5 ft (1.5 m) tall, so Starr estimated the men to be about 3 ft (0.9 m) tall, but said

The interiors of alien spacecraft are typically described as having smooth, metallic surfaces and rounded windows.

that they were otherwise quite human. They seemed to be wearing jackets that flared at the waist and square helmets that carried a reddish light on top.

Mrs. Starr opened her window and leaned out to get a better look. At this point a third figure came into view through the windows. Then the light inside was switched off and the outer skin of the object began to glow with a dull blue color. What looked like a wire antenna then rose out of the top of the object and began to emit sparks.

After about 5 minutes, the antenna slid back into the object, which began to glow more brightly. The UFO then took off as a row of small, circular lights appeared around its center line. After clearing the yard fence, the object tilted up and accelerated out of sight.

The Moreland Encounter

The Morelands had a small farm near the town of Blenheim, New Zealand, on which they grew some crops and kept cattle and other livestock. On July 13, Mrs. Eileen Moreland got up at her usual time of 6 am and went out to milk the cows before sending them out to pasture. The cow barn stood several hundred feet away from the house, on the far side of a paddock.

Eileen Moreland apparently witnessed green lights traveling through the sky above the cow barn of her New Zealand farm.

Mrs. Moreland's Account

The following is based on Mrs. Moreland's description of what happened next. As she walked across the field she noticed that a greenish glow was illuminating the low clouds as if an aircraft were shining a searchlight on them from above. Suddenly, two bright green lights burst from the clouds and dived down toward the farm. Mrs. Moreland watched them approach.

She thought there was something decidedly unpleasant about the shade of green. "It was a horrid sort of color," she reported later. "My first thought was, 'I shouldn't be here,' and I made a dive for the trees on the other side of the paddock."

From her shelter, Mrs. Moreland watched the lights get closer, and then realized that they were in fact attached to the underside of a large, dark gray object that she had not seen in the dawn gloom. The object was round, about 30 ft (9 m) across, and perhaps 10 ft (3 m) tall. It came to a halt, hovering some 15 ft (4.5 m) above the ground and 40 ft (12 m) from Mrs. Moreland. As it hovered, a series of yellowish-red spurts of fire burst out from its rim. Mrs. Moreland assumed these to be jets keeping the craft in position. There was a constant hum the whole time, and the object seemed to be radiating heat.

Mrs. Moreland then saw a glow on top of the craft. This seemed to be a light coming from a round, transparent dome. Inside the dome were two humanoid figures. The figures appeared to stand about 6 ft (1.8 m) tall and were dressed in close-fitting suits of a silver metallic fabric. Both men wore helmets that rose like cylinders from their shoulders to a flat top.

One of the men stood up and leaned forward as if staring out of the dome to study the farm and barn. He then sat down again, and the jets grew brighter and the hum increased in pitch. The object tilted to one side and then climbed up to disappear back into the clouds. It left behind a noxious smell similar to burnt pepper.

Investigating the Incident

Mrs. Moreland was deeply unnerved by what she had seen. She waited in the trees for some time, and when the object did not reappear she gingerly went to the barn and began milking the cows. She soon stopped, however, and went to wake her husband and tell him what she had seen.

The police were called at 7 am. They took the incident seriously and were soon on the scene. They found no marks or traces on the ground, but investigations soon turned up another witness. A man in Blenheim had seen the green object diving down from the clouds and then climbing again. He had not wanted to report the sighting, but did so when he heard of Mrs. Moreland's encounter.

EYEWITNESS ACCOUNT

THE FIGURES IN THE CRAFT

Mrs. Moreland described the two "men" she saw in the craft. According to Moreland, they were "dressed in fairly close-fitting suits of shiny material....I could not see their faces. One of the men stood up and put two hands out in front of him, as if leaning over to look downwards. He then sat down and, after a minute or two, the jets started off again and, tilting slightly at first, the thing shot up vertically at great speed and disappeared into the clouds. When it did this, it made a soft but high-pitched sound."

The Milakovic Encounter

On November 20, 1968, the Milakovic family was driving toward the village of Hanbury in Staffordshire, England, when they saw several rabbits bolt out of roadside vegetation and across the road. The Milakovics later said that they looked at where the rabbits had come from and saw a brightly shining object in the field.

The object, according to them, was shaped like a wide bowl with a transparent dome placed on top. From within the dome came varying white, orange and green lights. They claimed to see several humanoid figures moving around inside.

Several beings were clearly visible inside the transparent dome of the mysterious craft allegedly seen by the Milakovic family.

Mr. Milakovic braked to a halt, and he and his wife climbed out of the car to get a better look at the object. The UFO then took off and flew over the road to hover on the other side of the car. As it passed, the Milakovics said they felt a wave of warmth, as if the UFO was extremely hot and radiating heat. The UFO then began to wobble from side to side and to move in a series of jerky, random jumps. Worried that the object was going out of control, the Milakovics got back into their car and drove off. The last thing Mrs. Milakovic saw as she glanced back was that the light had grown more intense and the UFO seemed to be climbing.

UFOs and Water

Many people who study UFOs think that aliens are interested in water, as many sightings have been reported over water. On June 24, 1977, Mr. A. S. Cruz was driving along the coastal road near the village of Boca Chica in the Dominican Republic when he saw a light out to sea. When the light began to move faster than a boat should, Cruz stopped to look. Cruz claimed that as the light came closer, he could see that it was a disk-shaped object that was glowing white and flying some 20 ft (6 m) above the water.

The object, he said, came to a halt and let down a tube that reached the sea surface. Cruz assumed that it was sucking up water. He then noticed that two windows had appeared near the edge of the UFO. Through each peered a face that, although human in overall shape, was distinctly odd.

TALE OF THE PARANORMAL

UNIDENTIFIED SUBMARINE OBJECT?

In November 1971 some Maltese fishermen were pulling nets into their boat some 20 miles (32 km) south of Malta when they suddenly became aware – so they later alleged – of a large, dark object floating on the water about 900 ft (270 m) away. The fishermen had not seen it arrive but thought that it was most likely a military submarine, though they had never seen one like this.

According to the men, a brilliant light then flashed out from the object, forcing the fishermen to look away. When they looked back they saw a number of small men, each about the height of a 10-year-old boy but otherwise apparently human, walking around on top of the object. Several of the men seemed to be wearing belts to which were attached tools or pieces of equipment of some kind. After a few minutes, the humanoids jumped through an opening in the object's hull and disappeared.

The bright light then returned, causing the fishermen to turn away once more. When they looked back, the object was gone. They reported the sighting, and it was categorized by some ufologists as a USO (unidentified submarine object). Many felt, however, that this was so similar to other UFO sightings that it should be classified simply as a UFO that had landed on water rather than on land.

Alien Files

WHAT IS THE CONNECTION BETWEEN UFOS AND WATER?

What these and other similar reports have in common is that the UFO is allegedly seen hovering low over a body of water, or apparently resting on it, while the crew seems to place a tube into the water. The tube is usually described as being not part of the UFO itself but attached to a separate mechanism. Interestingly, the witnesses almost invariably state that the UFO sighted was sucking water up from the sea or river, but there seems to be no evidence to support this. If we are to believe the descriptions given, they might be discharging waste material or even pumping some sort of chemical into the body of water for reasons of their own. Some people have suggested that the UFO might need water to function correctly, while others think the water may be for the aliens themselves.

The UFO, Cruz said, lifted its tube and began moving toward the shore. Cruz got back into his car intending

Alien crafts' mysterious use of water remains a subject of debate among the UFO-watching community.

to drive off, but it would not start. Another UFO, similar to the first, now came into view and both moved to hover over Cruz's car. After a few terrifying moments, the UFOs flew off. Soon after that, Cruz was able to start his car.

River Incident

On March 22, 2001, Vinicius Da Silva and Marta Rosenthal were driving along the banks of the Tocantis River in Brazil after a day's fishing. Da Silva, who was driving, felt a sudden bump, as if they had driven over an object lying in the road, and braked to a halt. He got out to see what he had hit and if it had done any damage to the car.

As he was peering at the road behind them, Da Silva heard Rosenthal scream. Looking around, he saw her pointing out toward the river. They both later claimed they saw, hovering over the water, a disk-shaped object with a flat upper side on which was standing a short humanoid figure about 4 ft (1.2 m) tall. They described the object as having a silvery metallic color with a dull luster to it.

The humanoid, they reported, was standing on the edge of the dish dangling what looked like a hose into the river. After a few moments, it pulled up the hose and climbed into the UFO by way of a small hatch. The UFO began to grow brighter and shinier and slowly climbed into the sky. It then accelerated sharply and shot out of view.

Aliens and Plants

While some UFO sightings suggest aliens are obsessed with water, according to other reports, they can also take a keen interest in Earth's flora. In November 1960, Jose Alves of Pontal, a town in rural Brazil, was fishing in the Pardo River when he saw an aircraft approach. According to Alves, it soon became clear that this was no ordinary aircraft. About 15 ft (4.5 m) across, it flew with a strange wobbling motion and had no wings, tail or engines.

The object, he said, came to rest close to him. A small door opened and out sprang three men. Each man was about 3 ft (0.9 m) tall, wore a tight-fitting white suit and had dark skin. Alves was by now convinced that he was seeing devils – he had never heard of UFOs or aliens – and stood frozen with fear. The small men scampered about picking leaves from trees and pulling up bunches of grass.

After a few seconds, they clambered back into their craft. The object then rose vertically into the air and flew off in total silence. As soon as it was gone from sight, Alves bolted back home to pour out his story to his priest and, later, when reporters came calling, to the local press.

When patrolman Lonnie Zamora set out on patrol, little did he expect to have a close encounter with the world of the unknown.

The Socorro Incident

On April 24, 1964, at around 5:45 pm, patrolman Lonnie Zamora was heading south from Socorro, New Mexico, in his Pontiac police car when he noticed a sudden flash of blue-orange flame in the sky to the west. The bright light was followed by the sound of a roaring explosion. Fearing that the nearby dynamite shack had exploded, he decided to investigate. The following is based on Zamora's account of what happened next.

He turned off the road onto a rough gravel track. As he dipped down into a shallow gully, the flame came again. It was shaped like a cone with the top narrower than the bottom. There was a plume of dust kicked up from around the base of the flame. The roar came again and lasted for 10 seconds, sounding a bit like a jet but descending from a high to a low pitch. Zamora had to try three times before his Pontiac managed to get a grip on the gravel and ascend the steep slope to get out of the gully. As he reached the top, Zamora saw an object standing on the ground some distance from the dynamite shack, which was intact.

Two Figures

Zamora at first took the object to be an overturned car and the two figures standing beside it to be a pair of youths who had crashed. The figures were wearing white overalls of some kind and may have had rounded caps or helmets on. They had apparently been facing each other, but one turned around to look at Zamora as the police car crested the hill. Zamora radioed back to his police station to report a possible car accident. Unable to drive any farther on the rough track, he got out and walked toward the object. The two figures had vanished.

This artist's impression is based on Zamora's description of the craft and beings he claims to have encountered.

The Object

He could now see that the object was not an overturned car at all, though it was about the same size as one. It was a whitish-silver color and was shaped like an oval standing on one end. The object rested on four legs. It was about 4 ft (1.2 m) across and perhaps 20 ft (6 m) tall. There then came two loud thumps as if somebody had slammed a door. Zamora later assumed that this was the sound of the two humanoids shutting their door after they got into the craft.

By this time Zamora was within about 75 ft (23 m) of the object. The roar then began again, getting gradually louder, and the blue-orange flame erupted from the base of the craft. Fearing for his life, Zamora turned and ran. He glanced back from a safer distance to see the object hovering on its flame above the ground. Next time he looked, the flame and the roaring had stopped. The object hung eerily motionless and then moved silently off toward the southwest before vanishing behind some hills.

Alien Files

ANALYZING THE TRACES

A prominent ufologist, Dr. Josef Hynek, was at the site two days later. He found burn marks on the ground where the craft had stood. Four deep rectangular marks were seen in the ground where heavy objects had pushed down into the dry soil. The marks were arranged as if on the circumference of a circle, as they would have been if there were four legs supporting a round object. Given the soil composition in the area, it was calculated that the object that made the marks must have weighed from 3 to 6 tons. Zamora was a witness who was highly respected by his colleagues. Hynek concluded that a real, physical event of an unexplained nature had taken place.

ALIEN ENCOUNTERS

Since the late 1940s there have been abundant reports from all over the world of strange figures being seen in, beside and close to UFOs. Most of these accounts do not provide much information as to what the alleged aliens are actually doing here. They come and go, but it is hard to say why. However, there have been some reported instances of aliens interacting with humans, and, if these reports are to be believed, they may offer clues about the aliens' intentions. The fact that the reports tend to be inconsistent and often contradictory leads many ufologists to conclude that there is more than one type of alien.

Encounter Near Hasselbach

In 1952 a German official named Oscar Linke was riding his motorbike with his 11-year-old daughter Gabriella near Hasselbach when one of the tires burst. As they walked along the road pushing the bike, Gabriella saw something in a clearing. She pointed it out to her father, who at first took it to be a group of deer in the long grass but then decided it wasn't. He left the road and went to investigate. The following is based on Linke's description of what happened next.

When he was about 100 ft (30 m) from the object, he saw two men dressed in silver-colored suits who were bent over and fiddling with something on the ground. One of the men had a light attached to a belt around his waist. Linke walked on until he was just 25 ft (7.5 m) from the men. He then saw, in a position where it was hidden from the road, a large circular object resting on the ground.

Linke estimated that it was about 50 ft (15 m) across and shaped like two frying pans placed rim to rim but without the handles. On top of the object was a cylindrical tower about 10 ft (3 m) tall. Around the rim of the object was a row of dull, yellowish lights, each one about a foot in diameter and spaced some 2 ft (60 cm) apart.

Seeing her father stop in surprise, Gabriella asked him what was wrong. Apparently hearing the girl's voice, the two men looked up and saw Linke. They quickly jumped into an opening on the tower and disappeared from view. The lights on the object grew brighter

Oscar Linke initially believed that the UFO he had encountered was a Russian secret weapon.

and turned green as a hum began to emanate from it. The tower slid down into the object as the lights turned red and the hum grew louder.

The object began to rise, and when it reached a height just above the trees, the hum became a whistle that grew in pitch and intensity until it was almost

EYEWITNESS ACCOUNT

LINKE'S STATEMENT

"I would have thought that both my daughter and I were dreaming if it were not for the following element involved: When the object had disappeared, I went to the place where it had been. I found a circular opening in the ground and it was quite evident that it was freshly dug. It was exactly the same shape as the conical tower. I was then convinced that I was not dreaming."

unbearable. The object then flew off at great speed to the north.

Sighting in New Guinea

In 1959, an encounter took place at the Christian mission of Boaini deep in the remote jungles of New Guinea. Just after dawn on June 21, Steven Moi, a local who worked at the mission, reported seeing a disk-shaped object fly overhead. He reported the sighting to the priest in charge, Father William Gill, who assumed he must have seen an aircraft of some kind. Five days later, as dusk closed in, mission worker Eric Kodaware saw a bright light to the northwest. The following is based on eyewitness accounts of what happened next.

The light came closer, increasing in size until it was about five times the size of a full moon. Gill was called out and had the object pointed out to him. He, in turn, called Moi to see if this was the same thing that he had seen. Moi confirmed that it looked similar. By this time 38 people had gathered to watch.

The object descended to about 700 ft (210 m) above the mission's sports field. It was a round disk with gently curving upper and lower surfaces and a flange around the rim. Some ten minutes after its first appearance, something could be seen moving on its upper surface. When this thing came close to the craft's rim it became evident it was a man. He was soon joined by three others. They seemed to be working on a large box that emitted a blue light. The men came and went several times over the next half hour, apparently working at various tasks.

After the men had disappeared for the final time, the object began to rise, climbing through the low clouds. As it passed through the clouds, it lit them up, and it continued to do so for some time afterward, as if it were hovering just above them. A while later the clouds cleared, and various small lights were seen moving about the sky. At this point Gill believed he had seen some sort of top-secret military aircraft – perhaps a helicopter or hovercraft. Both the Australian and American military had bases in the area, and their aircraft regularly flew over New Guinea.

Father William Gill reported having a close encounter with aliens in a remote village in New Guinea in 1959.

Return Visit

The UFO apparently returned the following evening at about 6 pm. This time it descended to a height of about 300 ft (90 m). Again the mission workers gathered to watch. When the men again appeared on the craft, Gill suggested that they wave a greeting. He waved vigorously as if signaling hello. To his surprise one of the men on the object turned to face him and waved back. Then Moi waved both his arms over his head, and the figure waved back with both arms. The men on the object then disappeared while the craft continued to hover. At 6:30 pm the mission cook called to announce that dinner was ready. After dinner, Gill and his team went back outside. The object had moved to hover about 1 mile (1.6 km) away. A short while later it flew off. The following evening some moving lights were seen, but the large UFO did not return.

It was only when thinking about the events afterward that Gill thought them odd. He wrote an account of what had happened and sent it to a fellow missionary, suggesting that the craft may have been a UFO and asking, "Do you think Port Moresby (the base of the government authorities) should know about this?" It took time for his account to reach the authorities, and it wasn't until 1961 that news of the alleged sighting filtered out to the wider world.

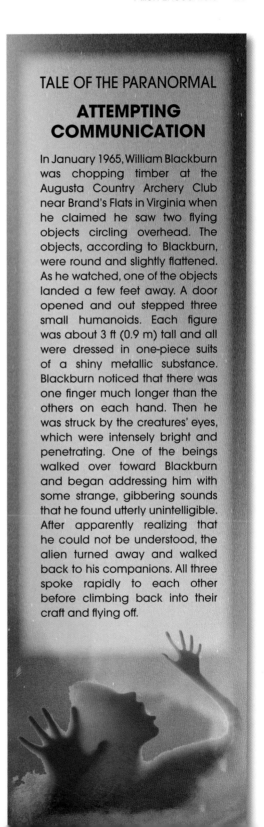

TALE OF THE PARANORMAL

ATTEMPTING COMMUNICATION

In January 1965, William Blackburn was chopping timber at the Augusta Country Archery Club near Brand's Flats in Virginia when he claimed he saw two flying objects circling overhead. The objects, according to Blackburn, were round and slightly flattened. As he watched, one of the objects landed a few feet away. A door opened and out stepped three small humanoids. Each figure was about 3 ft (0.9 m) tall and all were dressed in one-piece suits of a shiny metallic substance. Blackburn noticed that there was one finger much longer than the others on each hand. Then he was struck by the creatures' eyes, which were intensely bright and penetrating. One of the beings walked over toward Blackburn and began addressing him with some strange, gibbering sounds that he found utterly unintelligible. After apparently realizing that he could not be understood, the alien turned away and walked back to his companions. All three spoke rapidly to each other before climbing back into their craft and flying off.

TALE OF THE PARANORMAL

HOSPITAL VISITATION

At 8 am on January 1, 1970, nurses Dorren Kendall and Frieda Wilson arrived for work at the Cowichan Hospital on Vancouver Island, Canada, to begin their morning shift. One of their first jobs was to check that all the patients in the ward were comfortable and then open the curtains to let in the pale winter sunshine.

According to Kendall, as she threw back the curtains of the third floor ward where she worked, she was astonished to see a UFO hovering barely 60 ft (18 m) away and slightly below her. The UFO, she later said, was shaped like a flattened disk with a transparent dome on top. Through the dome Kendall could clearly see a pair of chairs facing what seemed to be an instrument panel. Standing behind the chairs and looking down at something out of Kendall's sight were two men dressed in dark clothing and helmets. As far as Kendall could see, the figures appeared to be human and about 6 ft (1.8 m) tall.

Kendall called out to Wilson to come quickly. At that moment one of the men looked up and saw Kendall. He tapped his colleague on the shoulder and began working the controls on the instrument panel. By the time Wilson had reached the window, the object was moving off but was still only about 100 ft (30 m) away. Together, the two nurses watched the UFO fly out of sight.

Carjacked

On the evening of November 2, 1967, Guy Tossie and Will Begay were driving south on Highway 26 near Ririe, Idaho. The following is based on their testimony of what they experienced in the course of their journey.

At around 9 pm, there was an unexpected flash of bright light from overhead and a flying object appeared ahead of them. The object was disk-shaped and about 9 ft (2.7 m) wide with a transparent dome on top that measured around 5 ft (1.5 m). The craft glowed with an eerie green color while orange lights flashed on and off around its rim. Within the dome two figures could be seen. Begay's car came to a gentle halt, its engine and lights cutting out as it approached the UFO.

The dome of the UFO flipped open and one of the figures jumped out, seeming to float down to the ground. It approached the car and opened the driver's side door, causing Begay to squirm across to join Tossie on the passenger's side. The alien got into the car and sat at the steering wheel without touching it. The UFO then began to move, apparently towing the car somehow as it began to roll off the road and into a recently harvested wheat field.

The two young men were staring in fear at the creature in the car with them. They described it later as being about 3 ft (0.9 m) tall with spindly arms and

legs but a very large, domed head. The head had huge, pointed ears flapping on either side and bulbous eyes fixed to the side of the head. The mouth was a thin slit and the nose was tiny. It appeared to be naked.

> *A significant proportion of alien encounters seem to happen to motorists as they travel on deserted roads.*

As the car bumped over the stubble, Tossie opened the door, jumped out and fled. He glanced over his shoulder to see that one of the creatures, carrying a light, was chasing him. Spotting a house, he leaped the garden fence and hammered on the door. The door was opened by farmer Willard Hammon, who would later describe Tossie as being so terrified that he could not talk.

After some minutes, Tossie calmed down enough to tell Hammon what had happened. Uncertain what to believe, Hammon set off to look for the missing Begay. Hammon discovered the car standing with its engine running and lights on in the middle of a field. Begay was cowering on the back seat with his eyes firmly shut and arms crossed over his face. Neither the aliens nor the UFO were anywhere to be seen.

Begay said that after Tossie had fled, the intruder had begun talking to him in an aggressive way as if it were angry. Begay had been unable to understand a word of what was said, describing the speech as being like that of a twittering bird. He had shut his eyes, expecting to be attacked at any moment. Instead he had heard the creature leave the car and walk off.

Paralyzed

The island of Isla de Lobos, off the coast of Paraguay, is home to a small base of the Paraguayan navy. At 10:15 pm on October 28, 1972, Corporal Juan Figueroa left the guardhouse to check the generator that powered the island's lighthouse. The following is based on his account of what happened next.

As he approached the generator hut, Figueroa noticed some dull, flashing lights beside it. He hurried forward in case something was wrong. Then he noticed that the lights were attached to a large, dark object resting on the ground beside the hut. The object was shaped like an upturned bowl about 18 ft (5.5 m) across, 10 ft (3 m) tall and with a dome or bulge on top of it.

TALE OF THE PARANORMAL

ENCOUNTER IN PERU

On February 3, 1972, Tito Rojas and Adolfo Penafiel were driving their truck through the semidesert landscape near Nazca, Peru. The following account is based on their own description of what happened to them.

They had reached a flat plain known as the Pampa Carbonera when the truck's radio was swamped with static. A few seconds later, the engine began to misfire, then stall completely. The truck coasted to a halt. Nearby, parked in the desert scrub, they saw what looked like a car. Thinking the driver needed help, Rojas and Penafiel walked toward it. As they drew closer they realized that the object was no car. It was, they later reported, an oval metal craft about 50 ft (15 m) long and 13 ft (4 m) tall, resting on three thick legs. It had a brightly polished silvery metal surface without any obvious joints, welds or openings.

Then a humanoid figure came into view. Dressed in a helmet and green suit, the figure was moving slowly and staring at the desert plants. It stopped now and then to bend closer or pluck a few leaves and twigs. As soon as it saw Rojas and Penafiel, the humanoid stopped in apparent surprise. Then it turned and quickly disappeared around the rear of the object. Seconds later the object began emitting a whine that grew rapidly in pitch and power. It then rose vertically and disappeared into the cloudless sky.

Figueroa saw there was a man standing next to it and a second man climbing down what seemed to be a ladder to join the first. He estimated that the figures were a little less than 5 ft (1.5 m) tall. A third figure, taller than the other two, now emerged from the dome and began to climb down. All three figures were dressed in dark, tight-fitting clothing and had their heads covered with helmets or hoods of some kind.

Realizing that these were intruders on the military base, Figueroa drew his pistol and shouted out a challenge. The three figures turned to face him, and the corporal felt a vibration or mild electric shock run through his body. To his alarm, he found he was paralyzed. A powerful voice inside his head seemed to be telling him not to shoot.

The three figures quickly climbed back inside the craft and shut the door behind them. The craft then rose into the air with a humming noise and hovered briefly at a height of about 120 ft (36 m). It then tipped upward, emitted a fireball and shot off at astonishing speed. Figueroa was instantly freed from his paralysis and ran back to the guardhouse to tell his story.

Tito Rojas and Adolfo Penafiel were driving through a remote area of Peru when they came across a UFO and its helmeted occupant.

Roswell

The reluctance of government officials to speak openly about alleged UFO sightings and apparent alien encounters experienced by military personnel has long been a source of great frustration to UFO investigators. In no case has this caused more friction, distrust and confusion than in what may well be the most famous reported alien encounter of them all: Roswell.

The Roswell incident took place in early July 1947. On July 8, a press release issued from Roswell Air Force Base by Lieutenant Walter Haut stated that a flying saucer, as UFOs were then known, had crashed near Roswell, New Mexico, and the wreckage had been recovered by

EYEWITNESS ACCOUNT

MAYBE IT'S A HOAX...

The editorial in the July 9, 1947, edition of the *Roswell Daily Record* read:

"What the disk is is another matter. The Army isn't telling its secrets yet.... Maybe it's a fluke, and maybe it isn't. Anyone's guess is pretty good at the moment. Maybe the thing is still a hoax, as has been the belief of most folks from the start. But, SOMETHING has been found."

The initial press interest in the Roswell incident was stifled by the release of this photograph, allegedly showing the wreckage from a weather balloon.

the military. A few hours later, a second press release was issued, stating that the wreckage was actually from a weather balloon. The mistake was explained as an error on the part of the personnel from Roswell who were unfamiliar with the new type of weather balloon that they had found. The air force displayed pieces from a weather balloon.

The Story Is Revived

With no further announcements, the press lost interest in the story, and the Roswell incident was to remain little known for decades. Then, in 1977, Jesse Marcel, who in the late 1940s had been intelligence officer at Roswell Air Base, told his account of events to two UFO researchers, Stanton Friedman and William Moore. Marcel told them that in July 1947 he had been sent out from Roswell to a nearby site to collect some debris that he was told had come from a flying saucer. He had done so and was ordered to take the wreckage to Wright Field, now the Wright-Patterson Air Force Base.

Marcel said that a press release had been issued, but that it was later quashed. He was stopped en route to Wright Field and ordered to hand over the wreckage to a senior officer, which he did. He was later told that the wreckage had actually been from a new type of weather balloon, but was unconvinced. For years, Marcel had remained unhappy with the weather balloon story but had been unable to prove anything.

Friedman and Moore obtained archive copies of the local newspapers and soon traced the names of the rancher on whose land the wreckage had been found, the local sheriff who had initially handled the investigation and several military personnel involved. They set off to track those people down and see what they had to say. By 1980, Friedman and Moore had interviewed 62 people. They were by then confident that something very strange had happened at Roswell and that the USAF had gone to great lengths to cover it up. The most likely explanation, they thought, was that a UFO had crashed and its wreckage had been recovered.

Dead Aliens?

In 1989 the story took a dramatic new twist when Glenn Dennis, who had worked as a civilian mortician in Roswell at the time, came forward to say that he had been told that bodies had been recovered from the crash. The air force medical team, he claimed, had phoned him to ask detailed questions about how to preserve bodies. He had later been threatened by the military to keep quiet. When news of Dennis's story became public, an air force photographer, who preferred to remain anonymous, came forward to announce that he had seen and photographed the bodies.

Alien Files

WAS THE ROSWELL UFO A MOGUL CRAFT?

By the 1990s, pressure was mounting on the authorities to provide some sort of explanation for what happened at Roswell in July 1947. In 1994, the USAF produced a report confirming that wreckage had been found at Roswell in early July 1947. It admitted that the wreckage had not been from a weather balloon. The second press release, it stated, had been a cover-up. The real story, this USAF report said, was that a craft belonging to the top-secret Project Mogul had crashed.

Project Mogul craft were ultra-high-altitude balloons, carrying highly advanced electronic equipment able to detect nuclear explosions. In effect, they were spy aircraft sent up to discover the secrets behind the Soviet atomic tests then taking place. The USAF report explained that in 1947 the need to maintain the secrecy of the Mogul flights had been paramount and so a cover-up had taken place.

Sequence of Events

It is very difficult to sort out the truth about what really did happen at Roswell. Most of the witnesses were speaking forty or more years after the event, and much of the evidence was not even firsthand. What can be said with some certainty is that something unusual happened in and around Roswell in early July 1947. The sequence of events has now been fairly clearly established as follows.

On Tuesday, July 1, the radar stations at Roswell Air Base and nearby White Sands, a missile testing base, picked up a UFO. It flew over very quickly and apparently performed maneuvers impossible for any known aircraft. However, the object was not actually seen. The following day, civilian residents of Roswell, Mr. and Mrs. Dan Wilmot, were sitting on their porch at around 10 pm when they allegedly saw an object flying west at high speed. They later described it as being shaped like two saucers joined around the rim.

On the evening of Friday, July 4, a radar-visual sighting of a UFO took place over Roswell while a thunderstorm raged. Local resident William Woody said he saw a white UFO with a red trail behind it flying northward over Roswell. Rancher W. "Mac" Brazel claimed he heard a loud explosion over his ranch but could not see anything. Farther north, Jim Ragsdale and Trudy Truelove were camping when they say they saw a craft fly overhead, apparently in trouble, and appear to crash a mile or so away near Corona. It has proved impossible to confirm whether these three reports relate to the same object. The witnesses could recall only that they happened late at night.

This contemporary illustration shows rancher Mac Brazel inspecting the strange metal wreckage on his land.

Meanwhile, the Roswell radar had again picked up an unidentified craft flying nearby. That object vanished abruptly, indicating either that it had crashed or that the trace had been a malfunction or one of several possible natural blips.

Early the next morning, Brazel rode out in the direction from which he had heard the explosion. He found strange debris scattered over an area about 2,100 ft (630 m) long by 600 ft (180 m) wide. Most of the debris consisted of a thin, silver-colored film that was both extremely light and very strong. There were also pieces of lightweight struts with an I-shaped section. Again these were very strong but, according to Brazel, some of them had odd markings that he later described as looking a bit like hieroglyphic writing. Brazel collected some of the debris and showed it to his neighbors.

Meanwhile, Glenn Dennis, the mortuary assistant, allegedly took a series of calls from Roswell Air Base asking for advice on preserving bodies. From what was said, Dennis got the impression that somebody important had been killed in an aircraft crash and that attempts were being made to make the mangled body look presentable. Then the military sealed off an area of land north of Roswell, near Corona.

On Sunday, July 6, Brazel took the pieces of debris to Sheriff George Wilcox, who called the Roswell Air Base to report the find. He seemed to think that if anything odd had fallen from the sky it was most likely something to do with the air force. Colonel William Blanchard, the base commander, sent Jesse Marcel to Wilcox's office to interview Brazel and collect the pieces of debris. The following day, Blanchard sent a team of men to Brazel's ranch to pick up all the pieces of debris and take them to Roswell Air Force Base.

On Tuesday, July 8, Blanchard told Lieutenant Walter Haut to write up a press release about the crash on the Brazel ranch. He was told to ascribe the wreckage to a "flying disk," which he did. The press release went out at 2 pm local time. Meanwhile, Marcel had set off for Wright Field with the wreckage bundled up in packing crates on board a B29. The aircraft made a stop at Fort Worth at about 4 pm, and Marcel was told to report to Brigadier General Roger Ramey. Ramey announced that the wreckage was no longer Marcel's responsibility and that he could go back to Roswell. Marcel handed over the packing crates and left.

At 5:30 pm Major E. Kirton issued a new press release stating that the "flying disk" of the earlier press release was a mistake. The debris had in fact come from a weather balloon. The FBI and air force then both moved quickly to repeat this version of events and so kill the story as far as the media was concerned.

The next day, July 9, more military personnel arrived at Brazel's ranch and picked up all the debris from the field, even the smallest fragments. Brazel himself was interviewed repeatedly by the military, which demanded to know every last detail of what he had seen and found. He was eventually released, though not before being

EYEWITNESS ACCOUNT

BRAZEL'S COMMENT

After the second press release came out, Mac Brazel said:
"I've seen weather balloons before, and I am sure what I found was not any weather balloon. But if I find anything else besides a bomb, they are going to have a hard time getting me to say anything about it."

instructed in very stern terms not to tell anyone anything.

The USAF Version

This much is agreed by almost everybody who has been involved in the Roswell incident. Most of it is even acknowledged by the USAF. According to the USAF version of events, the bang heard by Brazel and the objects seen by others was a Project Mogul craft exploding (see panel on page 28) and showering its remnants on the Brazel ranch to form a field of debris. The wreckage Brazel found was the remains of the Mogul craft. Neither Marcel nor Blanchard had ever seen such a craft, nor even knew of its existence, so they were at a loss to identify the wreckage.

The USAF claims that it only made the link between the reports coming in from Roswell and the missing Mogul on July 8. When the link was made, Ramey stepped in to take the wreckage from Marcel, and Kirton spread the false story about a weather balloon. The subsequent efforts to clear the Brazel land of debris, to clamp down on news and to silence Brazel himself are explained as efforts to maintain the secrecy of Project Mogul.

Years after the initial reports from Roswell in 1947, word began to leak out that a UFO had crashed and alien bodies had been found within.

In itself the USAF version makes sense, but it fails to explain the sighting of a flying object in trouble by Ragsdale or why a stretch of land some miles north of the Brazel ranch was sealed off for several days. Project Mogul was declassified a few years after the crash, but the incident at Roswell remained top secret. Why, researchers wonder, was the incident kept quiet if the project it was supposedly protecting was already in the public domain?

The Ufologists' Version

Ufologists, such as Friedman and Moore, offer an alternative timeline of events, based on their own research and interviews with witnesses. They suggest that the explosion heard by Brazel was a UFO suffering a severe malfunction, perhaps being struck by lightning. This explosion caused parts of the UFO to shower down into the debris field. The UFO then flew on northward erratically and probably out of control, crashing into a hillside off Pine Lodge Road near Corona.

The radar trace gave the authorities at Roswell the approximate site of the crash, and the next morning personnel were sent out to secure the area and search it. The crashed saucer was found at around 7 am. The military did not know of the debris field on the Brazel ranch until they got a phone call from Sheriff Wilcox, whereupon Marcel was sent to temporarily seal the area. He would later be replaced by more trusted personnel.

Various witnesses have testified to seeing a crashed object near Corona, others to seeing dead bodies of humanoid creatures about 4 ft (1.2 m) tall. Accounts differ somewhat as to the size and shape of the crashed UFO and to the appearance of the aliens. The UFO is generally reported to have been a dull silver color and to have been shaped like a crescent rather than a saucer.

This model is a recreation based on accounts of an alien being secretly dissected in the wake of the Roswell incident.

Alien Files

WHAT HAPPENED TO THE UFO?

Most of the evidence for Roswell was collected decades after the event, and not all of it was firsthand. Incidents may have been forgotten or exaggerated over time. If the stories are true, one has to ask: what has happened to the UFO and its occupants since? And if the USAF really did capture a sophisticated alien spacecraft, it would have been expected to grasp at least some of its secrets, yet USAF technology remains entirely Earth-based and explicable.

Some suggest that there was a central fuselage. The aliens are described as being basically humanoid. The bald heads were large in proportion to their bodies, with highly domed foreheads. The eyes were large, the noses small and the mouths mere slits. The wreckage and bodies were reportedly taken to Wright Field for future study.

Nordic Types

UFO researchers who have studied eyewitness descriptions of aliens have come to realize that most of these reported aliens fit into one of a small number of types. Among the first of these to be reported in any number are the Nordics. These aliens were given this name as they tend to be very humanlike and almost invariably tall with long blond hair and blue eyes, similar to the popular image of Scandinavians. They are usually seen dressed in one-piece, tight outfits that are described as being like ski suits or motorcycle leathers.

The Nordics are generally reported to behave in an aloof or detached fashion. They stare at the humans who see them and sometimes seem to take notes or talk about the humans. Some witnesses report that the Nordics seem friendly. Reports of the Nordics were most frequent during the 1950s and 1960s, but they declined in number during the 1970s and have never really become numerous again.

In the 1960s several Europeans reported meeting aliens with a humanlike appearance; they have since been dubbed "Nordic."

Goblin Types

Very different are the "Goblin" types. UFO experts say that these aliens are short, usually around 3 ft to 4 ft (0.9 m to 1.2 m) tall. Although they are described as humanoid in that they walk upright on two legs and have two arms and one head, they are otherwise bizarre in appearance. According to witnesses, they generally have long arms that end in claws or talons, large heads with grotesquely pointed ears and eyes that are reported to look evil or malevolent. Some Goblin types are reported to be covered in dense hair or long fur, but most are naked with smooth or reptilian skin.

The behavior of the Goblin types is apparently as aggressive as their eyes would indicate. They are prone to attack humans, inflicting cuts and scratches, and sometimes seem intent on dragging humans into their spacecraft. They are usually, but not always, said to be much stronger than their size would suggest. According to most reports, there is a noticeable lack of any technology or implements when compared to other alien types. Perhaps fortunately, reported sightings of these Goblin types have always been rare.

Grays

Ufologists call the most common type of reported alien the Gray. According to witnesses, these beings stand just under 4 ft (1.2 m) tall and are humanoid in appearance. They have thin, almost spindly, arms, legs and bodies, but very large and rounded heads. The arms and legs are sometimes said to lack elbows or knees and to end in long fingers and toes that are opposable but again lack clearly defined joints.

The heads are hairless and often earless and noseless. The mouths

Alien Files

TRICKSTERS

UFO researchers believe that the "Trickster" type of aliens are seen more often than either the Nordics or the Goblins. According to witnesses, these aliens appear to be broadly similar to humans, though they rarely stand more than 3 ft (0.9 m) tall. They are often said to wear one-piece suits and sometimes helmets or face masks. Tricksters are frequently reported to be deeply interested in plants and animals, especially crops or domestic livestock. They have allegedly been seen taking samples from plants and attempting to catch animals.

If witnesses are to be believed, the Tricksters, like the Nordics, seem somewhat uninterested in humans and react as if the arrival of a human is a bit of a nuisance. Sometimes they run away or take off in their UFO. At other times they will motion for the human witness to leave. If that does not work, they may paralyze or incapacitate the human, often with a tool that emits a beam of light.

are usually described as being mere slits, if they are mentioned at all. It is the eyes that seem to be the most noticeable feature of this type of alien. They are invariably described as being extremely large, jet black and almond-shaped. Some witnesses report them to have hypnotic powers, while others believe that any telepathic communication they receive is by way of these mesmeric eyes.

The behavior of the Grays is generally reported as unfriendly. Like the Tricksters they sometimes take an interest in plants and animals, but unlike the Tricksters they are very interested in humans. Attacks by Grays are generally more sophisticated than the physical violence of the Goblins but are nonetheless disturbing. They will try to induce humans onto their craft for a variety of unpleasant purposes including, as we will see in Chapter 7, abduction and medical experimentation.

A few witnesses have seen Grays accompanied by taller aliens. These tall Grays are around the height of a human and seem to be in command. Some witnesses describe them as being tan, rather than gray in color.

The Grays were first reported in North America. They were seen in small numbers during the 1950s and 1960s. During the 1970s sightings of the Grays increased dramatically, and by the 1990s there were more reports of Grays than of all other types of aliens put together. They remain the most regularly reported by witnesses.

The Kelly-Hopkinsville Encounter

On August 21, 1955, Bill Taylor was visiting his neighbors, the Sutton family, at their remote farm outside the small town of Kelly near the city of Hopkinsville, Kentucky. At around 7 pm Taylor went

Alien Files

ROBOTS AND BOUNCING BLOBS

As well as humanoid aliens, other types have been reported that owe little or nothing to human anatomy. Robots are, perhaps, the most numerous of these beings. Ufologists say they tend to be of metallic appearance and often have flashing lights attached to their bodies.

A final category goes by various names, such as "Exotic" or "Bizarre," depending on the researcher involved in categorizing them. The category includes all sorts of odd and unusual alien reports. Some witnesses have seen disembodied brains, headless birdmen or bouncing blobs of jelly. Most aliens in this category are only reported once.

out to the farmyard to get a bucket of water from the well. As he returned to the house he claims he saw a strange disk-shaped UFO flying low some distance away. It trailed an exhaust that seemed to be made up of gases of various colors. As Taylor watched, the UFO halted, then floated down to disappear behind a line of trees and apparently land in a dried-up riverbed. Taylor hurried back into the house to tell the six adults and several children of the Sutton family about what he had seen. They did not believe him, and Taylor dropped the subject. The following is based on Taylor's and the Suttons' descriptions of what happened next.

About an hour later, the farm dogs began barking loudly. Taylor and Elmer Sutton left their supper to go to the kitchen and look out across the farmyard. They both saw on the far side of the yard a most bizarre apparition. The figure they saw was about 3 ft (0.9 m) tall, walking upright on short legs and with very long, apelike arms. The creature's head was disproportionately large with enormous pointed ears, bulging eyes and a slit-like mouth. Even more unnerving was the soft, silvery glow that it emitted from its body. The being was joined by several more that then began to wander around the farmyard.

Elmer and Taylor picked up their guns and emerged from the kitchen doorway. Elmer shouted a challenge

The aliens that attacked the Sutton family farm had an appearance similar to storybook goblins.

to the beings. One of the aliens then turned toward the two men and ran at them with its arms held above its head. Elmer Sutton did not hesitate. He raised his shotgun to his shoulder and blasted the creature at point-blank range. The impact of the shot knocked the creature backward. It lay motionless on its back for a moment and then scrambled to its feet and ran off, seemingly uninjured.

On the Roof

The two men went back into the house and slammed the door behind them, while the rest of the Sutton family crowded into the kitchen to find out what was going on. Peering out of the windows, Taylor said he thought the creatures had gone, but then footsteps were heard on the roof of the house. Once more Taylor and Elmer ventured out with their guns. As Taylor stepped out of the door, one of the aliens grabbed his hair in its long, spindly hands. Whipping round, Taylor shot the alien with his rifle. It flipped backward over the roof and then seemed to recover and fled into the darkness. Elmer had meanwhile spotted one of the creatures squatting in the branches of a tree. He shot it, watching it jerk back from the branch and then float gently to the ground before it, too, ran off.

Besieged

Once more the men retreated to the house, this time barricading the doors and windows. For the next three hours the family remained – terrified – inside the house while the men took potshots at the aliens whenever they appeared. The family noticed that when hit by bullets or shotgun pellets, the aliens made a sound rather like a stone being thrown hard into an empty metal bucket. The strange glow of the creatures would increase whenever a shot was fired, only to fade quickly back to normal.

In the wee hours of the morning they decided to head for Hopkinsville Police Station. After they told their story, the police set off for Sutton farm. All was quiet when the convoy arrived. There was no sign of the aliens or of the UFO. The farmhouse and farmyard, however, did bear the marks of intense battle.

EYEWITNESS ACCOUNT

"SOMETHING FRIGHTENED THESE PEOPLE"

Elmer Sutton was known in the area as a cool, tough farmer, not given to flights of fancy. The Suttons' story seemed outlandish, but the local police were inclined to take it seriously. Chief of Police Russell Greenwell later commented: "Something frightened these people. Something beyond their comprehension."

Windows were smashed, doors were unhinged and surrounding trees and outhouses bore the clear marks of the shots fired during the siege.

Over the next few days the story spread rapidly, and it grew in the telling. Soon hundreds of people were flocking to see the site of the "great alien battle." Understandably, the Sutton family quickly tired of having strangers wandering over their farm. Elmer blocked access and chased off sightseers with threats. Yet despite suffering ridicule, the Suttons and Taylor never changed their story. They remained convinced that they had come under attack that night and had been lucky to escape with their lives.

Encounter at Valensole

Maurice Masse was a farmer in Valensole, France. On July 1, 1965, his day began normally enough. He rose at 5 am, ate a quick breakfast and climbed into his tractor to start work in his lavender fields. At about 6 am Masse stopped his tractor for a cigarette break. He heard a strange whistling noise that came from the other side of a small hill. Jumping down from his tractor, Masse trotted around the hill to investigate. The following is based on his description of what happened next.

Masse saw an egg-shaped object of gleaming silver metal mounted on six thin metal legs and a thick central support. It was about the size of a small van. Of more immediate interest to Masse were what he took to be two boys around eight years old who were pulling at a nearby lavender plant. They had their backs to him.

Thinking he had finally caught the vandals who had recently been attacking his lavender crop, Masse crept toward them. When he was about 15 ft (4.5 m) from the "boys," one of them seemed to hear him. The figure stood up and turned around and then quickly whipped out a small gun-shaped object and pointed it at Masse. The farmer stopped in alarm, but his alarm turned to fear when he realized that he had been paralyzed and could not move.

While Masse watched, the second figure also stood up. Masse could now see that they were not boys at all but bizarre entities.

Each figure stood about 4 ft (1.2 m) tall, with thin, slender bodies and limbs. The figures were dressed in tightly fitting green overalls, and they were wearing short boots on their feet. The creatures' heads were oval and completely bald, with a pointy chin and a small nose and ears. Their eyes were large and oval in shape and slanted upward. Their mouths were thin slits without lips.

This artwork is based on the descriptions given by Maurice Masse of his 1965 encounter.

The figures made some strange grunting noises, which Masse took to be their speech. Strangely, the mouths did not move, the sounds seeming to come from the throat area. The figure that had first seen Masse returned the gun-shaped object to a pouch attached to the side of his belt. With a final look at the lavender, the two figures moved toward the egg-shaped object. A sliding door on the side opened, and the figures entered. They did not climb in but seemed to float up from the ground.

The door slid shut, and the object began to emit the whistling noise that had first attracted Masse's attention. There was a dome on top of the object. A window appeared in the dome, and Masse saw one of the figures

Main image: *Maurice Masse owned a lavender farm.*

Inset image: *An investigator scrapes up samples from the soil at Masse's alleged UFO landing site.*

peering out at him. Then the window closed. The object rose vertically into the air to a height of about 60 ft (18 m). The whistling noise then stopped, and the craft disappeared off into the distance, toward the nearby village of Manosque.

For the next twenty minutes Masse's paralysis continued, and he feared he might die. When the feeling returned, he began walking, then running, for the village of Valensole. There he met the owner of the local cafe and blurted out his story. The cafe owner called the police.

The official investigation that followed collected evidence competently, including details of damage to the lavender and drawings of the marks left by the craft. It was noted that the plants around the landing site died in

EYEWITNESS ACCOUNT

SIMILARITIES WITH SOCORRO

Some years after the incident at Valensole, a French UFO investigator sent Masse a drawing of the UFO that had landed at Socorro, New Mexico (see pages 16–17), as he thought it sounded similar. Masse's reaction was immediate and emphatic: "That is what I saw," he replied. "You see, I was not dreaming and I was not mad."

the following days. Those farther from the spot where the craft had allegedly landed recovered, but those that had been under the craft did not. Masse himself claimed to feel unusually tired for several days.

Trickster Types

The aliens themselves fit the category that is now referred to as "Tricksters" (see panel on page 34). Their reportedly pallid skin, slanting eyes and pointed chins are typical, as are the rounded, bald heads and tightly fitting costumes. Their behavior is also similar to that described in other reports of this type of alien, including their interest in plants, particularly crops, and their strange floating movements as they boarded their craft. Similar to other reports, they were neither hostile nor friendly to the humans who saw them. UFO experts think the aliens did not want to be disturbed and took prompt action to disable Masse as soon as they became aware of his presence but otherwise left him unharmed. This behavior is apparently typical of Tricksters.

That Masse should have described beings so similar to those reported in other encounters is hard to explain. This is particularly the case since he lived in one of the most rural parts of France and had previously demonstrated no interest in UFOs, nor ever read or seen a science fiction book or movie.

ALIEN CONTACT

Some people have claimed not only to have encountered the occupants of UFOs, but to have spoken with them. Sometimes the conversation allegedly takes place in the language of the human who encounters the beings; at other times it involves miming or some form of telepathic communication.

Airship Encounters

One of the earliest such encounters occurred outside Homan, Arkansas, in 1896. It took place during a rash of sightings of mysterious airships over the US that year. James Hooten, a railroad engineer, was out hunting in the woods near Homan when he is alleged to have heard a loud whooshing noise that reminded him of an air brake on a steam locomotive.

Pushing through the undergrowth, Hooten emerged into a clearing. Resting there, according to his later testimony, was a large cigar-shaped craft with four paddle-like objects projecting out of the back and three large wheels along the side. A cabin hung down from underneath the strange craft to touch the ground. At the back of it stood a short man wearing a dark face mask. Hooten strolled up to the man and asked, "Is this the airship?" The man seemed surprised to see Hooten, but replied: "Yes, sir. Good day, sir."

There then followed a brief conversation in which the strange man told Hooten that the airship was powered by compressed air. Four other men then appeared and one said, "All ready, sir." The strange men quickly ran inside the cabin. The wheels began to turn and the object emitted a whooshing or hissing sound. It then rose into the air, accelerated to high speed and shot out of sight.

A few months later, in April 1897, J. Ligon and his son, of Beaumont, Texas, were walking home across farmland one evening when they saw a light in a field. According to their later account, they went to investigate and found a large, dark object with four men standing beside it. One of the men asked Ligon for water, and Ligon pointed out a nearby stream. The men said that they were flying their airship from the Gulf of Mexico to Iowa and that the craft was powered by condensed electricity. Once the water

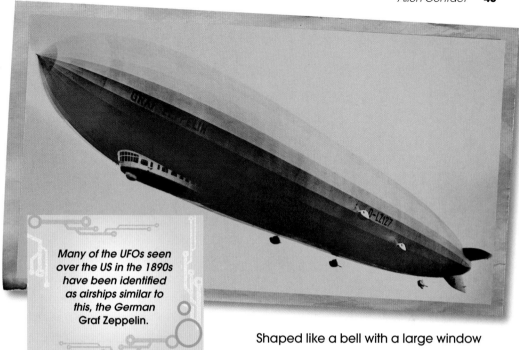

Many of the UFOs seen over the US in the 1890s have been identified as airships similar to this, the German Graf Zeppelin.

was acquired, the men entered the craft by a door and then took off.

Although Hooten and the Ligons interpreted their sightings to be of the mysterious airship seen over other parts of the US, their reports included features that would later appear regularly in accounts of alien contacts. The vague and ultimately meaningless descriptions of motive force would prove to be recurrent features.

Mental Images

In October 1959, Gideon Johannson had a power outage at his rural house in Mariannelund, Sweden. He and his son went outside to see if there were any obvious problems and, according to their later report, saw an unusual flying object behaving in an erratic manner.

Shaped like a bell with a large window on one side and glowing white, the UFO rocked from side to side, changed direction abruptly and crashed through the branches of a tree before coming to rest, hovering a short distance away.

Alien Files

WHAT WERE THE MYSTERIOUS AIRSHIPS?

During the waves of airship sightings in 1896–7, there were many attempts to explain what they were, including suggestions of hoaxes, pranks, publicity stunts and hallucinations. One man argued they were swarms of lightning beetles misidentified by observers. It is certainly likely that many reports were exaggerated by newspapers to increase sales. It has also been proposed that they were, in fact, human-built airships. These were rare at the time, but there is evidence that some were being flown around the US during the 1890s.

Johannson went to investigate and was 10 ft (3 m) from the object when he suddenly noticed two humanoids through the window. He stopped abruptly when he realized that the beings had also seen him. The figures were short with dome-shaped heads and pointed chins, but their main features were their eyes. These were large, dark and beautiful.

One of the beings used its eyes to transfer mental images to Johannson. These urged Johannson to stay where he was and showed the figures doing work on their craft, apparently repairing it. Johannson did his best to communicate back by thought or by waving, but the aliens studiously ignored him. After some minutes the UFO rose into the air, hovered and then emitted a bright flash, after which it was gone.

When the power engineers came to repair the power outage, they found that the lines leading to the Johannson house had been damaged about a mile away. Johannson believed that the UFO had inadvertently hit the cables, causing it to fly erratically and then come down to hover while the crew repaired the damage.

Alien Pancakes

Farmer Joe Simonton claimed to have achieved successful nonverbal communication with aliens during his alleged encounter with a UFO near his home at Eagle River in Wisconsin. The incident, which occurred on April 18, 1961, began as a fairly typical UFO close encounter. Simonton later said he heard a rumbling sound and, on leaving his house to investigate, saw a silver-colored oval craft about 30 ft (9 m) across and 12 ft (3.7 m) high, flying over his house.

The object came down to land a short distance away. Suddenly a hatch opened on top of the object, and three humanoid heads emerged. One of the figures climbed out. It was around 5 ft (1.5 m) tall and dressed in a tight-fitting outfit with a belt around the waist. The fabric was very dark blue, almost black, and seemed to be made of rubber or some such material. The creature's head was very human-looking with its straight, short black hair and swarthy complexion.

The alien had in his hand a large jug. He mimed as if drinking from the jug, from which Simonton concluded that his visitors were thirsty. He took the jug, filled it in his kitchen and brought it back. As he handed over the jug, Simonton peeked into the craft through the hatch and saw one of the aliens apparently frying something in a pan over a sort of stove. Simonton pointed to the pan and mimed eating food. The alien understood, picked up four pancake-like objects and handed them over to Simonton. The alien then closed the hatch and the UFO flew off, leaving

Gideon Johannson claims that the creatures he saw had strikingly large, dark eyes.

Simonton with the pancakes.

The farmer phoned the local authorities, who passed the details on to the UFO researcher Dr. J. Allen Hynek.

By the time Hynek and his team made contact with Simonton, he had eaten one of the pancakes. It was, he said, fairly unpleasant, having a taste and consistency like that of cardboard.

Alien Files

WHAT WERE THE PANCAKES MADE OF?

Hynek sent one of the other pancakes off for analysis. This showed it to be made of wheat bran, soya bean husks, buckwheat hulls and vegetable fats. In other words, it was from Earth.

Encounter in Brazil

Another successful attempt at mimed communication allegedly occurred on July 23, 1947. That day, José Higgins, a Brazilian surveyor, was working in a rural area near Pitanga. He had with him a team of local workmen to do the manual tasks. As they trampled over an open field, the men apparently heard a piercing whistle from overhead. They later said they looked up to see a large disk-shaped flying object diving down toward them. The workmen promptly threw down their equipment and fled, leaving Higgins alone. The following account is based on his description of what happened next.

As the disk neared the ground, a series of metallic poles came down to serve as landing legs. The object was, Higgins thought, about 150 ft (45 m) across and 15 ft (4.5 m) tall. There were windows set into the hull and through these Higgins could see two faces peering at him.

A flap fell down from the underside of the craft to form a ramp, and out walked three humanoid figures. Each figure was about 7 ft (2.1 m) tall and dressed in a tightly fitting suit of some plastic-type material. Each carried a metallic backpack and wore sandals. They looked like humans, although their legs were too long in proportion.

One of the figures waved at Higgins and then beckoned him over. Rather apprehensively, Higgins approached. The alien then pointed into the hatch. Higgins peered in, seeing only a small, empty room with a closed door apparently leading deeper into the UFO. The humanoid pointed again, and Higgins realized that he was being invited in, perhaps to go on a journey. He spoke to them in Portuguese,

José Higgins watched from the undergrowth after fleeing from the aliens that he says were trying to abduct him.

asking where they would take him. When the aliens showed no signs of understanding, Higgins resorted to making signs with his hands and exaggerated facial expressions.

Come with Us to Orque

Finally one of the beings seemed to understand. He pointed at the sun and said "Alamo," and then drew a circle in the sand and repeated "Alamo." He then drew seven circles around the sun, with a dot on each. He then pointed at the outermost dot and said "Orque." He pointed to Higgins, then to the UFO and finally to the seventh circle saying "Orque" again.

Higgins had no intention of being taken to another planet, but he did not want to try to outrun or outfight three alien beings, all clearly taller and stronger than himself. He got out his wallet and showed them a photo of his wife. He again used signs to indicate that he wanted to get her so that she could join them on the journey to Orque. The aliens nodded.

Higgins then strolled off as casually as he could manage. Once on the far side of the field he dived into woodland, squirmed into a hiding place inside undergrowth, and then turned to watch events. The aliens spent the next half hour or so wandering around, looking at plants, throwing stones and seeming to waste time while awaiting the return of

Higgins. Perhaps finally losing patience, the aliens then reboarded the UFO. The hatch slammed shut and, with the same whistling noise it had made earlier, the UFO took off and flew out of sight.

TALE OF THE PARANORMAL

SIGN LANGUAGE

After sunset on December 31, 1974, a farmer in Vilvorde, Belgium, was walking across his yard when he was surprised to find the whole area suffused in a pale green light. He then saw a humanoid figure about 4 ft (1.2 m) tall walking across the far side of the yard. The figure had what looked like a knapsack on its back and was holding a vacuum-cleaner-like object, which it was swinging back and forth as if using it to scan the ground. When the farmer shone his torch on the intruder, it turned to face him and moved its hands rapidly as if using sign language of some kind. Finally, it gave up trying to communicate, climbed over the wall and left the yard. A few seconds later, the farmer heard a hissing sound and a disk-shaped UFO rose from behind the wall, emitting a shower of sparks. It hovered for a short time and then flew off at high speed.

Montana prospector Udo Wartena apparently gave permission for an alien to extract water from a mountain stream.

was familiar with the various army aircraft that flew overhead and assumed that this was one flying closer to the ground than usual. The following account is based on his description of what happened next.

Turning to face the direction of the noise, Wartena saw what he took to be a military aircraft. It was hovering about 600 ft (180 m) away, above a stream that meandered through a meadow. The craft was large. Wartena later estimated it to be about 100 ft (30 m) long and shaped like a lens, with the central section about 35 ft (11 m) thick.

"Just Like Us"

As Wartena watched, he saw a section of the hull drop down to reveal a spiral staircase. Down the stairs came a

Encounter in Montana

When the aliens show that they can speak the language of the witness, it makes communication much easier than with gestures and sign language. One such encounter apparently took place in May 1940, though it did not become public until some years later.

Udo Wartena was working on his small gold claim in a remote valley near Townsend, Montana, when – so he later claimed – he heard a loud rushing noise, like that of a turbine. He

humanlike figure dressed in a gray uniform with a cap. The new arrival began approaching Wartena, so the prospector strolled forward. The figure waved at Wartena, and as they got to within 10 ft (3 m) of each other, he asked if it would be all right to take some water from the stream. Wartena said it was. The stranger then turned and waved back to his craft. A hose came down from the hovering UFO to dip into the stream.

The man then invited Wartena on board his craft. Still thinking that he was dealing with the US military, Wartena agreed. He climbed the spiral stairs to find himself in a room about 12 ft by 15 ft (3.5 m by 4.5 m). The room was lit by a pale light, the source of which Wartena could not see.

In the room was an older man seated on a plushly padded bench. Wartena asked why the men wanted water from his small stream when there was a large lake not far away. The younger man replied that it was because the stream water was purer and contained no algae.

Wartena had now realized that although the man spoke good American English, he was doing so slowly and stumbling over certain words as if this were not his native language. In May 1940, war was raging in Europe and Asia, and Wartena suddenly became suspicious of where these men were from, and so

he asked them. "We are from a different planet," came the reply. "It is a long way from here." Wartena was surprised, to say the least, by this response but felt totally at ease with the aliens. They were "just like us, and very nice," he later reported.

Wartena asked his new alien friends why they had come to Earth. He was told that they had been visiting Earth for some years to gather information, leave instructions and help out when they could. They then invited Wartena to come with them, but he declined, saying that his friends and family relied on him and he could not just go wandering off without telling them.

Alien Files

SKIPPING OVER LIGHT WAVES

Wartena claimed that the younger alien explained to him how their craft worked. The alien said that there were two flywheels around the rim of the craft that spun in opposite directions. This gave the craft an internal gravity negating that of Earth or any other planet. The craft gained its power by focusing the gravitational energy of whatever celestial body was the closest and then using this to skip over the light waves faster than the speed of light. They claimed to be able to store small amounts of the gravitational energy for emergency use.

At this the two men ushered Wartena off the UFO. They told him to get well away from the craft before it took off and not to discuss the event with anyone. In the event, Wartena did not move off far enough. The rushing noise began again, and the rim of the UFO began to spin. It lifted vertically off the ground, hovered for a few seconds while wobbling slightly and then flew off. As it left, Wartena collapsed. His muscles simply would not work and did not return to normal for more than an hour.

Visitors from Cassiopeia

In September 1955, Josef Wanderka was riding his moped through woods near Vienna, Austria, when – so he later reported – he came upon a silvery egg-shaped object resting in a clearing. A door in the side of the object was open, and a ramp led down to the grassy glade. Gingerly, Wanderka entered the object to find himself in a large, featureless room, where he was confronted by six humanoids.

The humanoids, according to Wanderka, were taller than him, and each had long blonde hair tied back in a bun or ponytail. He likened their faces to those of children. They were dressed in one-piece garments that reached from the neck to the wrists and toes. Taken aback, Wanderka stammered out his profuse apologies for having entered the craft, introduced

The aliens that farmer Gary Wilcox claims to have met were fascinated by his tractor.

himself and began backing out of the door.

One of the humanoids then began talking in German with a slight accent. It urged Wanderka not to leave, assuring him that he was in no danger. The alien said that they had come from the star system Cassiopeia and asked Wanderka how things were on Earth. This being the height of the Cold War, with Austria caught between the Soviet and capitalist areas, Wanderka blurted out a quick summary of the current international tensions.

The alien suggested that perhaps Wanderka could become Earth's leader and sort the problems out. Wanderka was wondering how to respond to this odd suggestion when the alien changed the subject and demanded to know how the moped worked. After Wanderka had explained, he was ushered out of the UFO, which then took off.

TALE OF THE PARANORMAL

FARM TALK

Gary Wilcox, a farmer from Newark in Newark Valley, New York, claimed that he found a strange object in one of his fields on April 24, 1964. Shaped rather like an elongated egg, about 20 ft (6 m) long and 4 ft (1.2 m) tall, it seemed to be made of a shiny, silver metal, all of one piece, without any signs of joints or rivets.

Wilcox apparently gave the object a kick. Suddenly two figures came out from underneath the object. They were about 4 ft (1.2 m) tall and dressed in white overalls that had a metallic sheen. Wilcox began backing away, but one alien called out to him, "Don't be alarmed, we have spoken to people before."

Wilcox later thought that although he could understand clearly what was being said, the figure had not actually been speaking English but had been making strange bubbling and moaning noises. The aliens asked Wilcox if he could explain how his tractor worked. Wilcox did so, and then he was asked what he was doing with it. He explained that he had been spreading manure on a field, but the aliens did not seem to understand the concept of fertilizer, so Wilcox went on to explain that as well.

The aliens said that their home planet was very rocky and unsuitable for growing Earth-type crops. They said that they preferred to visit rural areas as the skies over cities were too polluted with fumes and gases that interfered with their craft's energy system. The aliens then disappeared back under the object. The object rose slowly and silently to a height of about 150 ft (45 m) before gliding off to the north.

George Adamski

George Adamski was a Polish-born American citizen who shot to international fame in 1954 with the publication of his book *Flying Saucers Have Landed*. The book, co-written by British writer Desmond Leslie, was based for the most part on Adamski's alleged encounter with a UFO in 1952. Adamski asserted that on November 20, of that year, he and some friends had been enjoying a picnic in the Mojave Desert when they saw a large, cigar-shaped UFO pass overhead, chased by some military jets. As the UFO fled, a smaller disk-shaped UFO seemed to detach itself and came down to land a mile or so away. While his friends waited, Adamski set off to investigate the landed flying saucer. The following is based on Adamski's description of what happened next.

As he approached, he was met by a humanoid who was dressed in brown overalls. The alien could speak no English but made himself understood by a mixture of hand signals and telepathy. The being explained that he had come from the planet Venus as a messenger to Earth. The Venusians were a highly advanced civilization but were deeply worried by the wrong turn that humanity had taken technologically by taking up nuclear power for both warlike and power-generating purposes. The Venusian said that not only was humanity at risk, but so were other interplanetary races, as the radiation was leaking out from Earth into space. The Venusian explained that he and his race wished to correct the path of humanity by peaceful means but warned that other races – from such planets as Jupiter, Saturn and interstellar

These two photographs were taken by George Adamski. He claimed that they were evidence that alien spacecraft had visited Earth.

planets – were not so well disposed and might resort to force if mankind did not change its path voluntarily.

The Venusian then asked to borrow a roll of photographic film that Adamski had on him. Adamski handed it over, whereupon the alien left.

Adamski hurried back to his friends with his news. They agreed to sign a statement confirming their viewing of the original UFO and the smaller saucer.

On December 13, Adamski returned to the desert to retrieve his film. He was visited by a flying saucer, the film dropping from a porthole. When developed, it showed a variety of spacecraft.

Men in Black

Some UFO witnesses claim that after their encounter they faced questions and threats from "men in black" – men, usually dressed in black suits who claim to be officials of secret organizations or government agents. They often threaten UFO witnesses to keep quiet about what they have seen. Some ufologists believe men in black are, in fact, aliens whose job is to prevent witnesses from talking about them.

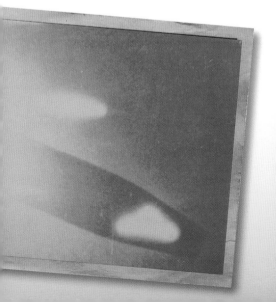

Alien Files

WAS ADAMSKI A FRAUD?

The book, and the photographs, created a sensation. Some believed Adamski; others condemned him as a charlatan. His background as part-time philosopher, self-appointed professor, one-time alcohol bootlegger and burger-stand salesman did not inspire confidence.

In 1955 two of the friends who had been at the fateful picnic came forward to say that in fact they had seen no UFO. They had signed the statement prepared by Adamski to help him sell the story for cash, but now that the story was becoming so widely believed, they felt that they had to retract.

In the years that followed, Adamski claimed to have been visited by the Venusians on several more occasions. He also claimed to have been taken to the moon and to Venus, where he found lush forested valleys. By 1960 his claims had become utterly outlandish and lacked any evidence to support them. The photos of spacecraft were proclaimed by experts to be clever fakes made by photographing detailed models in carefully controlled artificial light.

Adamski died in 1965. Soon afterward space probes would reveal that the planets he claimed to have visited were quite unlike his descriptions, and their environmental conditions made them incapable of supporting life, let alone advanced civilizations.

One of the earliest reported men in black episodes took place in 1954 when UFO investigator Albert Bender was at home in Connecticut. Bender was head of the International Flying Saucer Bureau and published a regular journal titled *Space Review*. He claims he was visited by three men dressed in smart black business suits and wearing black, homburg-style hats. They kept the hats pulled down so that the brims partially hid their faces. One of them was carrying a copy of *Space Review*. After standing around in ominous silence for some time, the men began communicating with Bender by telepathic means. They told him that he had to stop his UFO investigations at once. They issued threats and made claims that terrified Bender.

The next day, Bender ceased publication of *Space Review* and resigned from the International Flying Saucer Bureau. He later moved to the West Coast of the US, cut off all contact with his friends and insisted on having an unlisted phone number. Thereafter several UFO witnesses, and some investigators, began reporting threatening visits from men dressed in black, or in official uniforms of one kind or another.

In November 1961, Paul Miller claims he saw a landed UFO and two humanoids in North Dakota. According to Miller, the following day he was visited in his office by three men in black suits who claimed to be from the government. They asked him detailed questions about the UFO and demanded to be shown the clothes that Miller had been wearing at the time. So frightened was Miller by the threatening behavior of the men that he drove them to his house and showed them the clothes. After inspecting them, the men left.

Empty Threats

In 1967, Robert Richardson reported sighting a UFO near Toledo, Ohio. According to Richardson, he saw it land and later picked up a piece of metal from the landing site, which he passed to a scientist for analysis. Three days later – so he claims – two men pulled

Alien Files

WHO ARE THE MEN IN BLACK?

Opinion is divided among UFO investigators as to who the men in black might be. Some ufologists believe men in black are in fact aliens, or androids controlled by aliens, sent out to cover up alien activity on Earth. Others think they are government agents seeking to hush up UFO sightings. A third theory is that they are hallucinations caused by the trauma of encountering a UFO. The truth is that nobody is entirely certain who the men in black might be. It is clear, however, that, as far as we know, none of their threats have ever been carried out and nobody has ever suffered at their hands.

In the 1997 film Men in Black, *a group of secret agents is tasked with the responsibility of protecting the Earth from alien invasion.*

up outside his house in a 14-year-old black Cadillac. They asked him a few innocuous questions about the UFO and then left.

A week later, says Richardson, two different men arrived in a different car. They wore black suits and spoke with foreign accents. They acted in a threatening fashion and sought to bully Richardson into accepting that the UFO sighting had been a mistake or dream. Then one of the men asked for the piece of metal. When Richardson said he no longer had it, the man

turned angry. "If you want your wife to stay as pretty as she is, you had better get that metal back," the intruder declared. Then both men left the house hurriedly. It subsequently turned out that both cars had fake license plates and that the metal was a fairly nondescript iron alloy. The men were never seen again, and their threats were not carried out.

This photograph taken by Jim Templeton in 1964 clearly shows a strange, unexplained figure behind his daughter.

had a lovely time and noticed nothing unusual, other than the fact that cattle in a nearby field seemed rather nervous and prone to galloping around for no apparent reason.

However, when Templeton got his photos developed, he was in for a shock. One of the photos he had taken of his daughter showed a strange figure in the background. The figure looked like a man dressed in a tight-fitting white suit with a visored helmet on his head and one arm on his hip. Templeton sent the photos and negatives back to the camera company for an explanation, but they could suggest no technical fault with the developing process that would have caused the background figure to appear. Yet Templeton and his family

Figure in the Photo

One case of men in black who did not utter threats came to light in 1964. On May 24, Jim Templeton took his family on a picnic on Burgh Marsh near his home in Carlisle, England. The family were adamant that no man in a space suit had been present. The photos were later given to the police, who likewise failed to explain them.

A few days later, Templeton claims he got a phone call from a man who said that he worked for the government and asked if he could come to interview him about the incident. Templeton agreed, and after a few minutes two men knocked on his door. They showed him apparently genuine papers identifying themselves as working for the military police.

After a few minutes' conversation about the incident, the two men offered to drive Templeton out to the site of the picnic. When they got to Burgh Marsh, the two "military policemen" apparently turned nasty. They began demanding that Templeton admit he had faked the photo or that an innocent passer-by had been present. Templeton refused, whereupon the two men left abruptly and drove off. Templeton had to make his own way home – a journey of about 5 miles (8 km).

The British military later insisted that the two men did not work for them and that they had no interest in the matter.

Hypnotist Threatened

Dr. Herbert Hopkins of Orchard Beach, Maine, was a professional hypnotist who used his skills to assist UFO researchers to probe the memories of

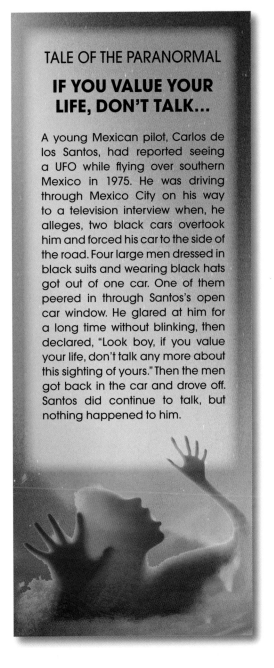

TALE OF THE PARANORMAL

IF YOU VALUE YOUR LIFE, DON'T TALK...

A young Mexican pilot, Carlos de los Santos, had reported seeing a UFO while flying over southern Mexico in 1975. He was driving through Mexico City on his way to a television interview when, he alleges, two black cars overtook him and forced his car to the side of the road. Four large men dressed in black suits and wearing black hats got out of one car. One of them peered in through Santos's open car window. He glared at him for a long time without blinking, then declared, "Look boy, if you value your life, don't talk any more about this sighting of yours." Then the men got back in the car and drove off. Santos did continue to talk, but nothing happened to him.

UFO witnesses. It is often claimed that people under hypnosis are often able to recall details that have been lost from their conscious minds.

In September 1976, Hopkins was helping with the witness David Stephens, who had allegedly seen a UFO the previous October. On September 11, Hopkins's wife and children had gone out for the evening when he received a phone call from a man claiming to be vice president of the New Jersey UFO Research Organization. The man said he was in the area and asked if he could drop by to discuss the Stephens case. Hopkins agreed. The following is based on Hopkins's description of what happened next.

Just moments later, the man arrived. He was dressed in an immaculate black suit with sharply creased trousers, black hat, black shoes, black tie, gray gloves and white shirt. Hopkins let the man in and asked him to sit down. The man removed his hat to reveal that he was totally bald and that his head and face had a pale, whitish color.

The two men chatted for some time about UFOs in general and the Stephens case in particular. Hopkins noticed that his guest spoke in a curiously flat, emotionless monotone. Odd as this was, even stranger was the fact that the man was wearing lipstick that came off on his glove when he brushed his lips with his fingers.

Suddenly the visitor stated that his host had two coins in his pocket. Hopkins checked, and it was true. He asked Hopkins to put one of the coins in his hand. Hopkins handed it over and watched in great surprise as it went out of focus and then vanished from the man's open palm. The man then said: "Neither you nor anyone else on this planet will ever see that coin again." He warned that he could make a heart vanish from within a human body, just as he had made the coin disappear. He ordered Hopkins to stop working on the Stephens case and to destroy all his files and information. By now thoroughly terrified, Hopkins agreed.

The man then began to slur his words. He stood up abruptly and announced: "My energy is running low – must go now – good-bye." Walking stiffly and with apparent difficulty, the man left the house and went out to the driveway. Hopkins saw a bright bluish light that he took to be a car's headlights.

EYEWITNESS ACCOUNT

HOW DID HE GET THERE SO QUICKLY?

After the telephone call, Hopkins went to the door to switch on the porch light so that his visitor would be able to find his way from the driveway. He was surprised to see a man already climbing the porch steps. Hopkins later said: "I saw no car, and even if he did have a car, he could not have possibly gotten to my house that quickly from any phone."

The man in black who visited Herbert Hopkins was able to make a coin disappear in eerie and ominous circumstances.

When Hopkins's family arrived home, he told his wife of his strange visitor. Together they inspected the drive and found odd markings unlike those that would have been left by a car or motorcycle. Hopkins quickly discovered that there was no such thing as the New Jersey UFO Research Organization.

Deeply worried about who, or what, his visitor might have been, Hopkins dropped the Stephens case and destroyed his files.

ALIEN ABDUCTIONS

No other type of alien encounter has attracted more attention in recent years than that of abduction. The nightmarish quality of the reports makes these stories perhaps the most dramatic and intense alien encounters yet reported. Although the details of the alleged experiences vary a great deal, they nearly all tend to fit into a pattern.

The Wolski Encounter

One morning in the summer of 1978, Jan Wolski, a 71-year-old Polish farmer, was driving his horse-drawn cart through the woods near his home. According to Wolski, on the road ahead of him, he suddenly saw two small humanoids. The beings, he later said, were about 4 ft (1.2 m) tall and very slender in build. They were dressed in tight-fitting one-piece outfits of a silver-gray color. Their heads were larger than a human's would have been in proportion to their bodies, and they had large, almond-shaped eyes of a very dark color. Their ears and noses were very small and their mouths little more than slits. Bizarrely, they were bouncing along as if their shoes contained hidden springs. The following account is based on Wolski's description of what happened next.

When Wolski came closer, the two creatures noticed him and

The creatures that Jan Wolski allegedly encountered had large heads and dark, almond-shaped eyes.

bounded over to sit up on the cart. One of them pointed forward along the lane, seemingly indicating that Wolski should continue. The two beings then chatted to each other in a language that Wolski did not understand. He did, however, get the very strong impression that the beings were in a jovial and happy mood. After a few minutes the cart entered a clearing, and the two beings jumped down. They began bounding off toward a UFO that was hovering above the clearing. The object was white and shaped like a house, with a pitched roof like that of a barn. At each corner were cylindrical objects from which projected vertical black poles topped by spinning spiral objects. A loud and intense humming sound filled the air. As Wolski watched, a black box-like object began descending from the UFO on four cables.

Entering the UFO

One of the humanoids then turned to Wolski and beckoned him over. Since he had felt no impression of hostile intent, Wolski climbed down from his cart and walked across the clearing to the UFO. The being then gestured for him to enter the box, which he did. The box ascended into the UFO. Stepping out of the box, Wolski found himself inside a very gloomy room. There were two large tubes extending from one side of the UFO interior to the other, and

a number of rods in the floor that Wolski took to be controls. Also on the floor were a dozen or so birds, apparently paralyzed or dead.

One of the humanoids indicated by hand signals that Wolski should undress, which he did. The aliens then studied Wolski visually and passed what seemed to be scanners over his body. He was then instructed to get dressed again and was shown back to the box-like elevator apparatus. The elevator descended with Wolski and the two aliens in it. After Wolski exited the elevator, the UFO rose slowly into the air before departing at high speed.

Alien Files

WHAT ARE ALIEN ABDUCTIONS?

Alien abductions are experiences – real or imagined – in which people are taken against their will by apparently nonhuman entities and subjected to physical and psychological tests. The first case to gain widespread attention was that of Antonio Villas Boas, a Brazilian farmer, who claimed to have been abducted by aliens in 1957. Since then there have been many hundreds of alleged cases, particularly in the United States. Do they really happen? Most scientists believe that alien abductions are in fact a product of fantasy, false-memory syndrome, hallucination, hypnosis and other psychological phenomena.

The Pascagoula Case

On the evening of October 11, 1973, two shipyard workers ran into the police station in Pascagoula, Mississippi, claiming that they had been abducted by aliens. Sheriff Fred Diamond did not at first believe a word of the story, but realizing that the men were clearly terrified, he agreed to take a statement. Both men, Charlie Hickson and Calvin Parker, told near-identical tales.

The men claimed they had been fishing from a pier in an isolated area off Highway 90. They had heard a loud zipping noise behind them and turned to see an oval-shaped object hovering about 3 ft (0.9 m) off the ground. The object was glowing with a pale blue light. A door opened in the side of the craft, and three humanoids came floating out. The figures were about 5 ft (1.5 m) tall and glowed with a soft white light. Their heads were high and domed with large, black eyes and slits for

Charlie Hickson and Calvin Parker were fishing in the Mississippi when they were abducted by three strange-looking aliens.

mouths. Their ears were small, conical and stuck out sideways from their heads. Their arms ended in clawlike hands with simple pincers instead of fingers. Both Parker and Hickson said that they thought the beings were robots rather than living beings.

One of the aliens grabbed Hickson by the shoulder, causing him to feel a strange stinging or tingling sensation. He then drifted into a trancelike state in which he was only vaguely aware of what was happening. Parker passed out completely at this point and was unable to remember anything.

According to Hickson, both men were levitated by the aliens and floated into the UFO. Inside the craft, the men were subjected to what appeared to be medical tests. Hickson recalled lying on a table while a gigantic scanning device shaped like an enormous eye was passed repeatedly over him.

"We Mean You No Harm"

The aliens then floated the two men back out to the riverbank and dumped them on the ground next to their abandoned fishing tackle. One of the beings then sent a telepathic message to Hickson, saying: "We are peaceful. We mean you no harm." Parker came to at this point, just in time to see the aliens leave and the UFO fly off.

By the time he had finished taking down the statement, Sheriff Diamond was skeptical. The story sounded too

bizarre to be true. He left the men alone in the interview room but continued to listen to what they said. He was half expecting the men to start gloating about how their hoax was fooling the police, but instead Hickson and Parker continued to talk about their encounter in worried tones (see panel).

Now confident that the two men were telling him what they believed to be true, Sheriff Diamond arranged for them to have a medical examination at a nearby USAF base. The doctor found no signs of any injuries, nor of radiation, though both men did have a small cut similar to that used when taking blood samples.

A couple of days later, Parker had a nervous breakdown and was admitted to the hospital. Hickson, however, remained able to answer questions. He took a lie detector test, which he passed, and then underwent hypnotic regression to see if he could recall any further details about the encounter, but little more was revealed.

Alien Files

WERE PARKER AND HICKSON REALLY ABDUCTED?

The case appeared to be a dramatic and impressive account of abduction by aliens. However, later investigations found that the lie detector test had not been carried out according to standard procedure, so the results could not be relied upon. Moreover, the man who was on duty that night at a toll bridge just 900 ft (270 m) from the site of the encounter was questioned and said he had seen nothing all evening.

Some UFO researchers chose to reserve judgment on the case, but others accepted that Parker and Hickson really were victims of an alien abduction that evening. The two men later turned down a movie contract that would have brought them a considerable sum of money, saying that they just wanted to forget the whole affair.

The Day Encounter

On October 27, 1974, the Day family were driving home to Aveley in Essex, England. They were in a hurry to get back in time for a television program Mrs. Sue Day wanted to watch, which started at 9 pm. According to the Days, as they were driving they saw an oval blue light in the sky. The light seemed to follow them for a while, but then disappeared. A few minutes later, as the car rounded a bend, it was engulfed by a green mist. The car radio at once began buzzing with static, and John Day, fearing a short circuit, disconnected it. There was a bump as if the car had run over an object. Then they came out of the mist and drove home.

While John reconnected the car radio, Sue took the children indoors and put them to bed. Then she went back downstairs to watch her TV show. But the show was not on – the screen was filled with static. After fruitlessly trying to get a signal, she glanced at a clock and was astonished to see that it was almost midnight. It was at least two and a half hours later than it should

have been. John could not explain the time lapse either.

Nightmares

In the weeks that followed, all the members of the family began to have nightmares in which there was a recurrent image of a monstrous face. The children were particularly terrified by the visions. Both John and Sue found themselves becoming increasingly interested in environmental issues, to which they had paid little attention before.

Eventually the nightmares got to be too much, and the Days consulted their doctor. He sent them to see Dr. Leonard Wilder, who specialized in trauma and sleep problems. Wilder thought that something may have happened during the missing time on October 27 that had inflicted trauma of some kind and that the Days had subconsciously blocked it from their minds to help them cope.

Wilder hypnotized both John and Sue to take them back in their memories to the night in question. The Days independently recalled almost identical tales. When the car had entered the green mist, the engine had first misfired and then died completely. Through the mist had then walked a group of aliens dressed in tight-fitting silver suits. These beings were over 6 ft (1.8 m) tall and generally human in appearance, except for the fact that they had catlike eyes of penetrating power.

According to the Day family, their car broke down as they entered a mysterious green mist.

These aliens escorted the Days from their car through the mist to the blue UFO and led them on board. Neither John nor Sue could recall any form of physical force being used. It was as if they had wanted to go with the aliens, perhaps in response to telepathic prompting of some kind.

Once inside the UFO the Days were handed over to a quite different group of aliens. These were about 4 ft (1.2 m) tall and dressed in white cloaks. They had animal-like faces with large eyes and pointed ears. It was these faces that had been haunting the dreams of the family. These creatures, the Days came to believe, were servants to the first group of aliens and had been

trained by them to perform various duties. One of these was to conduct physical examinations of humans. The Days were then examined each in turn by the animal aliens.

Environmental Message

Once the medical tests were over, the taller aliens reappeared. They showed the family around the UFO, which was arranged on three decks. The aliens then told the Days that their home world was under threat of devastation by runaway pollution and other environmental threats of a less specific nature. They showed them a holographic film of their home planet and the threats it faced.

Although it was not specifically stated, the Days got the impression that the aliens had been visiting Earth to study humans for some considerable time. It also seemed that the aliens were carrying out tests or experiments that involved genetics or children in some way.

The Days then recalled being led back out of the blue UFO and through the green mist to their car. John started the engine and they set off. The moment they came out of the mist, their memories of the incident were wiped clean.

The Godfrey Encounter

On November 28, 1980, police officer Alan Godfrey was driving near the town of Todmorden in Yorkshire, England, when he saw a UFO with a domed upper side and flat underside hovering over the road in front of his police car. He stopped and pulled out his notebook to sketch the object. The next instant he was parked by the side of the road about 750 yards (800 m) away with no idea of how he had gotten there. A quick glance at the dashboard clock showed that it was now 20 minutes later.

Godfrey drove back to where he had seen the object to find that the road surface where the UFO had hovered was dry, although all around the

EYEWITNESS ACCOUNT

GODFREY'S TESTIMONY

During his hypnotic testimony, Godfrey described some of the details of his strange experience. He said he remembered being in a strange room, more like a house than a spaceship, complete with a most unexpected large black dog. Yoseph was described as aged about 50, with a long beard and wearing "biblical" clothing. Assisting Yoseph were several small robot-like creatures about the size of a five-year-old child and with a head shaped like a lamp.

ground was wet from recent rain. He later discovered that the sole of his boot was split.

After reporting the incident, Godfrey at first refused to talk to UFO researchers, but six months later agreed to hypnotic regression as he was by then eager to know what had happened during the missing minutes.

Under hypnosis, Godfrey told how a beam of light had shot out from the UFO as he prepared to sketch it. He had then fallen unconscious, coming to in a room lit dimly by some light source that he could not see. He was lying on his back on a hard table or platform. Beside him stood a human-looking male. The man explained that his name was Yoseph, or something similar, and that he was not going to harm him, just carry out a few tests.

Godfrey then became aware of several smaller figures that he took to be robots. These figures milled around him, shining lights and prodding him with instruments that gave him severe head pains. When the robots backed off, Yoseph returned. He said that Godfrey could now leave but that they would meet again at some point. Godfrey was then returned to his car, though he was not clear exactly how, and he then woke up as he had remembered.

The Platner Encounter

Julio Platner was driving his van along a rural road near Winifreda, Argentina, on August 9, 1983. It was not yet dark when he claims he saw a bright, bluish light hovering over the road ahead of him. According to Platner's later testimony, he stopped the van and got out to try to get a better look at whatever the object was.

He was suddenly hit by a beam of brilliant light that dazzled him and sent him stumbling backward. He remembered falling, then came to, lying on a flat, hard table in a dimly lit room. The room was about 10 ft (3 m) across with curved walls that glowed slightly. Moving around him were four humanoid creatures. For some reason that he could not really explain, Platner thought that one of the aliens was a female. Platner tried to sit upright but was held firmly in place by one of the aliens gripping his shoulders. He tried to scream, but no sound came from his mouth.

One of the aliens came over to stare at Platner with its huge black eyes. Platner then received a telepathic message telling him not to worry as the aliens would not harm him. "What you are experiencing now," the Gray continued, "has happened to thousands of other people. When it is over you can talk of this if you like. Some people will believe you, but most will not."

After this communication, Platner became calmer and more relaxed. The female came over with a long, rigid tube that she filled with blood from Platner's arm. Further tests and medical examinations followed, lasting about

Alien Files

WHAT DID THE ALIENS LOOK LIKE?

The aliens, as described by Platner, appear to fit into the Gray category. The figures were basically human in shape, though their limbs and bodies were slender and rather elongated. They stood just over 4 ft (1.2 m) tall and were a pale grayish-white color. Platner was not certain if they were naked or dressed in very tight clothing. Their heads were entirely bald with domed foreheads. Their noses, mouths and ears were tiny, but their eyes were huge and bulging without any eyelashes.

the female Gray had extracted blood.

The Weiner Encounter

In 1988 Jim Weiner sustained a head injury and during the medical recovery process he underwent hypnosis. While in this state, Weiner revealed that he, his brother and two friends had seen a UFO while on a camping trip back in 1976. Jim's brother Jack, Chuck Rak and Charlie Foltz all subsequently agreed to be questioned about the experience.

They each recalled that they had been canoeing and camping in the Allagash River area for a few days in August 1976. On the 26th they had camped beside East Lake. As dusk fell, they had paddled out to fish the lake waters to catch their supper and that was when they saw a large, round object hovering some distance off to the southeast. When Foltz switched on an electric torch, the object had swooped toward them. A beam of light flashed out in the direction of the young men. The next thing they could remember, they were standing on the lake shore about three hours later. The UFO was flying away.

An alien Gray looms out of the mist. Many witnesses have reported being enveloped by a fog as the abduction takes place.

20 minutes. Platner was then told to stand up and was given his belongings. He then passed out once again. When he recovered consciousness, he was lying on top of the roof of his van about 1 mile (1.6 km) from where he had encountered the UFO. On his left arm was a small wound at the spot where

Under separate hypnotic regression each of the men told a broadly similar story of what had happened during the missing hours. The men recalled that as the beam of brilliant light hit the canoe they had panicked and then been overwhelmed by lethargy and tiredness. They had then floated upward along the beam of light toward the UFO. Passing into the craft they had

Alien Files

TYPICAL FEATURES OF ALIEN ABDUCTIONS

1. **Missing time.** Almost all witnesses discover, after encountering a UFO, that there is a period of time missing from their memory.
2. **Nightmares.** Commonly, witnesses experience nightmares, visions or some kind of mental disturbance following the encounter.
3. **Hypnotic regression.** This leads witnesses to undergo hypnotic regression in order to find out what happened during the missing time.
4. **Abduction.** Hypnosis recovers apparent memories of being abducted, more or less unwillingly, by aliens.
5. **Medical examination.** Witnesses typically recall that, once inside the UFO, they were laid out on a table and subjected to physical examinations, which are frequently painful.
6. **Departure.** Witnesses are often given a tour of the UFO and then allowed to leave, retaining no memory of the experience.

been confronted by a group of aliens matching the usual description of Grays. The Grays had used some form of mind control directed through their eyes to force the men to undress.

The men were then sprayed with a fine mist-like gas before being forced to lie down on tables. They were then subjected to a series of studies and investigations of an apparently medical nature. Painful probes were inserted into their bodies to extract samples of blood and skin. Throughout all this the Grays seemed utterly indifferent to the feelings and pain experienced by the four men.

The men were then allowed to get dressed. The Grays returned and, again using telepathic coercion, forced the men to walk through a circular doorway. They were engulfed by the light beam once more and transported back to their canoe. The young men paddled ashore, clambering out as the UFO took off, which was when their conscious memories took over.

The Interrupted Journey

The encounter reportedly experienced by Betty and Barney Hill took place in 1961. However, it was not generally known about until the publication in 1966 of *The Interrupted Journey*, a best-selling book based on the incident. The Hill encounter began on September 19, 1961, when Betty and Barney were returning from a vacation

in Canada. They were driving down Highway 3, hoping to arrive home in Portsmouth, New Hampshire, by around 3 am.

At about 11 pm, while passing Lancaster, the couple claim they saw a bright light in the sky that seemed to be flying north at high speed. It then turned suddenly and moved southwest at a slower pace. The Hills drove on for a few miles, with the object seeming to keep pace with them, though it was moving in an erratic manner.

About halfway between Lancaster and Concord, the Hills pulled over and got out of their car to watch the object. It came down closer. According to the Hills, they could now see that it was an oval-shaped, bluish-white object with a row of windows on its leading edge and two projections on either side. Through the windows they could see diminutive humanoids trotting about as if attending to some mission or other.

A red light appeared on each projection, and Barney later claimed he suddenly took fright. He insisted that his wife get back in the car as he was convinced that "they" were going to attack. The Hills got back in their car and drove off at high speed. Although they heard beeping noises and what seemed to be stones hitting their car, they soon left the UFO behind and drove on through the night. They returned home at around 5 am and went straight to bed.

TALE OF THE PARANORMAL

AGEIST ALIENS

On August 12, 1983, Alfred Burtoo says he was sitting enjoying a quiet evening's fishing beside a canal in Berkshire, England, when he saw a light circling overhead. Assuming this to be a helicopter, Burtoo took little notice. He poured out a cup of tea from his flask as he watched the "helicopter" land a short distance away. Two short men left the object and began walking toward Burtoo, whose dog got up and began snarling. The figures were about 5 ft (1.5 m) tall and dressed in green overalls with headgear rather like motorcycle helmets with visors covering the face. The men asked Burtoo to accompany them. Burtoo put down his tea and followed them.

He climbed a short flight of steps into the UFO, having to duck his head as the doorway was very low. Once inside, Burtoo was bathed in an orange light for a few seconds. Then one of the figures asked him how old he was. Burtoo replied that he was 77. There was a hurried conversation between the two figures, after which one of them announced: "You can go now. You are too old and infirm for our purposes." Burtoo was hurriedly pushed out of the craft. The door was slammed shut behind him, and the UFO began to rise silently into the air as Burtoo went back to finish his cup of tea, which was now lukewarm.

Five days later Betty Hill wrote a letter to UFO investigator Donald Keyhoe outlining what had happened. A few weeks later Keyhoe and his team contacted the Hills and on November 25, they visited them to get a detailed version of the encounter. It was during this process that the Hills realized that there was a time discrepancy. They had stopped for only a few minutes to look at the UFO, and yet were two hours late getting home.

The matter did not end there. Barney's account was soon found to be riddled with inconsistencies. Although he was adamant that he had seen the crew of the UFO only at a distance and indistinctly, he also reported that the leader of the crew had an expressionless face and that another crew member had grinned at him when looking back over his shoulder.

It was Betty, however, who was to have real problems. Over the following months, she had a series of vivid nightmares. These contained disjointed and terrifying images linked to the UFO encounter. She saw herself undergoing very painful medical tests, being marched into the UFO by uniformed aliens, talking in English to the aliens, and being shown a star map. The jumble of scenes emerged gradually over a long time.

Hypnotic Regression

Barney meanwhile began to suffer from depression and lethargy as well as a nasty stomach ulcer. His doctor thought that he might be suffering from mental issues related to accumulated past experiences that had become too much for him to cope with. Barney was therefore sent to see Dr. Benjamin Simon who specialized in hypnotic regression, in order to expose and thereby deal with the causes of his emotional problems.

After a few sessions with Barney, Dr. Simon asked Betty to attend a session. He conducted several hypnotic regression appointments with the two separately before revealing what he had found. Under hypnosis, the Hills had told almost identical stories.

Under hypnosis, the Hills stated that they had seen the UFO much as previously described. But as Barney drove off, the car was stopped by a dozen men standing in the road. The men had opened the car doors, reached in and pulled the Hills out. The Hills, who were strangely unable to struggle or resist, although both were very frightened, were then escorted by the men into the woods and to a clearing where the UFO was resting on the ground.

Top: *Betty and Barney Hill are seen here shortly after their abduction experience.*

Above: *This artist's impression shows Alfred Burtoo's supposed attempted abduction.*

The Hills described the aliens as being around 4 ft (1.2 m) tall and basically human in proportion, but their heads were large and oval-shaped with pointed chins, snub noses and slit-like mouths. Their eyes were large and slanted, and they did not seem to have any external ears. They were dressed in tight-fitting suits of black leather or some other smooth fabric. Some of them had small peaked caps on their heads.

Medical tests

According to the Hills, they were marched up a ramp into the UFO itself. Barney's recollections became vague at this point, but Betty was able to recall events clearly. She was taken to one room, and Barney to another. In the room Betty met an alien who could speak good English. He asked

Betty Hill says that she was given a tour of the alien craft, and was shown a star map.

Betty questions about her age, diet and physical health and then took samples of ear wax, hair, fingernails and skin scrapings. The man then asked Betty to lie on a couch and attached her to a large machine equipped with needles, dials and gauges. He began an extremely painful examination that involved jabbing needles into her, apparently to see if she was pregnant. Another of the aliens then entered and waved his hand, at which point the pain left Betty. The new arrival then asked to look into Betty's mouth and seemed surprised that she could not take her teeth out. Betty explained that Barney had false teeth. This led to a conversation about the aging process in humans.

Star Map

The new arrival, whom Betty took to be the leader of the crew, then talked to her for some time, seemingly fascinated by the fact that Barney had black skin and Betty white. He also showed Betty a map of the location of the star system from which he said they had come. Betty asked for some proof of the aliens' existence and the leader handed over a book, but it was soon taken away when other members of the crew objected. The leader then told Betty that neither she nor Barney would remember anything of the event, adding that even if they did, nobody would believe them. The Hills were then

marched back down the ramp and returned to their car. The UFO took off and the Hills continued their journey back home.

Alien Files

WHAT IS OUT THERE?

The sheer number of reports of alien encounters from different parts of the world, and the similarities between them, make the phenomenon hard to dismiss as nothing more than imaginary. Yet even if some of the stories are true, we don't know for sure that the creatures described in them are aliens. In fact, as skeptics point out, interstellar travel would take centuries, even at light speed, so the chances of visits from other habitable planets are actually pretty low. Other theories have been proposed, such as that they are visitors from another dimension, or time-travelers from Earth's future. Yet most scientists continue to believe that alien encounters are hallucinations. They point to the fact that alien appearances have changed over time according to fashion, from the beautiful "Nordics" of the 1950s and 1960s, to the more science-fiction "Grays" of today. Similar experiences were being described in the 19th century as encounters with trolls or fairies. So is it just something about the human mind that sometimes causes us to think we have experienced something otherworldly? Or is there really something out there? We can only look at the evidence and decide for ourselves.

GLOSSARY

abduction The act of forcibly taking a person or persons away against their will.

airship A lighter-than-air, power-driven aircraft kept buoyant by a body of gas.

anonymous (of a person) Not identified by name; of unknown name.

antenna A rod, wire or other device used to transmit or receive radio signals.

atomic tests Tests of nuclear weapons.

bulbous Fat, round or bulging.

circumference The enclosing boundary of a curved shape, especially a circle.

debris Scattered fragments of something wrecked or destroyed.

depression Severe despondency and dejection.

diameter A straight line passing from side to side through the center of a shape, especially a circle or sphere.

discrepancy A lack of compatibility or similarity between two or more facts.

erratic Not even or regular in pattern or movement.

extraterrestrial Of or from outside Earth or its atmosphere.

false-memory syndrome A condition in which a person's identity and relationships are affected by memories that are factually incorrect but strongly believed.

FBI The Federal Bureau of Investigation, an agency of the U.S. government that has responsibilities for gathering intelligence and investigating crime.

flange A flattened rim that stands out around the edge of an object.

flying saucer A popular term for UFO.

fuselage The main body of an aircraft.

gauge An instrument for measuring the magnitude, amount or contents of something.

Goblin A type of reported alien. Goblin-type aliens are short with long arms that end in claws, large heads and pointed ears. They are known for their strength and aggression.

gold claim A piece of land on which an individual hoping to find gold has the right to mine.

Gray The most common type of reported alien. Grays are short with spindly arms, legs and bodies. They have large rounded heads, extremely big, dark eyes and are known for abducting humans and experimenting on them.

gully A water-worn ravine.

hallucination An experience involving the apparent perception of something not present.

hieroglyphic writing A type of writing that uses symbols.

hoax A deception.

humanoid Having an appearance resembling that of a human.

hypnosis The induction of a state of consciousness in which a person apparently loses the power of voluntary action and is highly responsive to suggestion or direction.

hypnotic regression A process of taking a person back to an earlier stage of life through hypnosis.

incapacitate Prevent from functioning in a normal way.

interstellar travel Travel between stars.

lie detector test A test to see whether someone is telling the truth. The test is usually carried out using a polygraph, a machine that detects and records changes in physiological characteristics, such as a person's pulse and breathing rates.

maneuvers Movements requiring skill and care.

mesmeric Hypnotic.

monotone A voice that is unchanging in pitch and without intonation.

mortician A person whose business is preparing dead bodies for burial or cremation.

Nordic A type of reported alien. Nordic-type aliens tend to be very humanlike, tall with long blond hair and blue eyes. They are described as behaving in an aloof, disinterested fashion toward humans.

noxious Very unpleasant.

paralyzed Partly or wholly incapable of movement.

phenomena (plural of phenomenon) Facts or situations that are observed to exist or happen.

prospector Someone who searches for mineral deposits, such as gold, by means of experimental drilling and excavation.

psychological Of, affecting or arising in the mind; related to the mental and emotional state of a person.

psychotherapy The treatment of mental disorder by psychological rather than medical means.

radiation Energy emitted as waves or particles.

Soviet Union A former federation of communist republics that occupied the northern half of Asia and part of eastern Europe between 1922 and 1991. After World War II it emerged as a superpower that rivaled the US and led to the Cold War.

spindly Thin and insubstantial.

star system A large number of stars with a perceptible structure; a galaxy.

telepathic communication The supposed communication of thoughts and ideas by means other than the known senses.

trauma A deeply distressing or disturbing experience.

Trickster A type of reported alien. Tricksters tend to look like humans, except for their short stature. They are allegedly very interested in plants and animals but less so in humans.

turbine A machine for producing continuous power in which a wheel or rotor is made to revolve by a fast-moving flow of water, steam, gas, air or other fluid.

UFO Unidentified flying object – a mysterious object seen in the sky for which, it is claimed, no scientific explanation can be found.

ufologist A person who studies UFOs.

ufonaut A traveler aboard a UFO.

USAF United States Air Force.

weather balloon A balloon equipped with special equipment that is sent into the atmosphere to provide information about the weather.

FURTHER INFORMATION

Aliens and UFOs by Christopher Evans (Carlton Books, 2008).

The Mystery of UFOs (Can Science Solve...?) by Chris Oxlade (Heinemann Library, 2006).

UFOs (Trailblazers) by David Orme (Ransom Publishing, 2006).

UFOs: Alien Abductions and Close Encounters (Graphic Mysteries) by Gary Jeffrey (Book House, 2006).

UFOs and Aliens (Amazing Mysteries) by Anne Rooney (Franklin Watts, 2009).

UFOs and Aliens: Investigating Extraterrestrial Visitors (Extreme!) by Paul Mason (A & C Black, 2010).

WEB SITES

Due to the changing nature of Internet links, Rosen Publishing has developed an online list of Web sites related to the subject of this book. This site is updated regularly. Please use this link to access the list:

http://www.rosenlinks.com/pfiles/ali

INDEX

Numbers in bold refer to illustrations.

Adamski, George 52-53

airships 42-43, **43**, 76

aliens
abductions by 35, 60-75, 76

behavior of 7, 11, 12, 13, 15, 16, 17, 18, 20, 21, 22-24, 25, 33, 34, 35, 36-38, 39, 40-41, 42, 44, 46, 47, 49, 52, 60, 62, 63, 66-68, 71, 72

blobs of jelly 36

clothing of 4, 9, 11, 13, 15, 16, 18, 21, 22, 24, 33, 39, 40, 41, 44, 46, 47, 49, 50, 51, 52, 56, **56**, 60, 65, 66, 68, 72, 74

dead 4-5, 7, **7**, 27, 30, 32, **32**

encounters with 4, 18-41, 42-59

Goblins 34, 35, **37**, 76

Grays 34-35, **35**, 36, 68, **69**, 69, 70, 75, 76

medical tests by 35, 61, 63, 66, 67-69, 70, 72, 75

Nordics 33, **33**, 34, 75, 76

photos of 56, **56**, 57

physical characteristics of 21, 22-23, 25, 33, 34-35, **35**, 36, 39, 41, 42, 44, 45, 46, 50, 51, 60, **60**, 62, 63, 65, 66, 68, 72, 74

sightings 4-5, 8-9, 12, 13, 18-21, 22-24, 25, 36, 39, **39**, 54

"talking" with 21, 24, 40, 42, 47, 49, 51, 52-53, 61, 67, 72, 75

Tricksters 34, 35, 41, 77

warnings by 52-53

Alves, Jose 15

atomic tests 28, 76

Begay, Will 22-24

Bender, Albert 54

Blackburn, William 21

Blanchard, William 30, 31

Boas, Antonio Villas 61

Botta, Enrique 4-6, 7

Brazel, W. "Mac" 28, 29, **29**, 30, 31, 32

Burtoo, Alfred 72

Cassiopeia 51

close encounters
of the second kind (CE2) 8

of the third kind (CE3) 6, 8, 18-41, 42-59

Cruz, A. S. 13-15

Day family 64-67

Dennis, Glenn 27, 30

Diamond, Fred 62, 63, 64

false-memory syndrome 5, 61, 76

FBI (Federal Bureau of Investigation) 30

Figueroa, Juan 24-25

Flying Saucers Have Landed 52

Friedman, Stanton 27, 32

Gill, William 19-21

Godfrey, Alan 67-68

Hammon, Willard 23

Haut, Walter 26, 30

Hickson, Charlie 62, **62**, 63, 64

Higgins, José 45-47

Hill, Betty and Barney 70-75, **73**

hoaxes 5, 26, 43, 63, 76

Hooten, James 42, 43

Hopkins, Herbert 57-59

humanoids. *See* aliens

Hynek, Josef Allen 17, 45

hypnosis 64, 65, 69, 70, 73, 76

International Flying Saucer Bureau 54

Interrupted Journey, The 70

Johannson, Gideon 43-44, 45

Kendall, Dorren 22

Keyhoe, Donald 72

Kirton, E. 30, 31

Kodaware, Eric 19

Leslie, Desmond 52

lie detector tests 64, 76

Ligon, J. 42

Linke, Oscar 18-19

Marcel, Jesse 27, 30, 31, 32

Masse, Maurice 38-41

men in black 53, 54-55, **55**, 56-59, **59**

Milakovic family 12-13

military aircraft and personnel 4, 19, 20, 26-33, 48, 49, 52, 57

Miller, Paul 54

Moi, Steven 19-21

Moore, William 27, 32

Moreland, Eileen 9-11

nightmares 65, 70, 72

"Orque" 47

Parker, Calvin 62, **62**, 63, 64
Penafiel, Adolfo 24, 25
Platner, Julio 68-69
Project Mogul 28, 31

Ragsdale, Jim 28
Ramey, Roger 30, 31
Richardson, Robert 54-55
Rojas, Tito 24, 25
Rosenthal, Marta 15
Roswell incident 26-33, **26**, **29**, **31**, **32**

Santos, Carlos de los 57
Silva, Vinicius Da 15
Simon, Benjamin 73
Simonton, Joe 44-45
Soviet Union 4, 28, 51, 77
Space Review 54
spies and spying 28
Squyres, William 6-8
Starr, Mary 8-9
Stephens, David 58, 59
Sutton, Elmer 36-38

Taylor, Bill 36-38
telepathy 42, 44, 52, 54, 63, 66, 68, 70, 77
Templeton, Jim 56-57
time-travelers 75
Tossie, Guy 22-24
Truelove, Trudy 28

ufologists 6, 13, 17, 18, 27, 32, 33, 34, 36, 41, 45, 53, 54, 57, 64, 67, 72, 77

UFOs 4, 5, 6, 7, 9, **9**, 24, 26, 61, 77
and water 13, 14, 15, **48**
bell-shaped 43
cigar-shaped 6, 8, 42-43, 52
disk-shaped/"flying saucers" 4-7, 8, 12-13, 15, 18-21, 22, 26, 27, 28, 30, 32, 36, 45-46, 47, 48, 50, 52, 53, 76
lights attributed to 8, 10, **10**, 12, 13, 16, 19-20, 21, 22, 24, 42, 47, 67, 68, 69, 71
noises attributed to 6, 7, 11, 16, 17, 19, 24, 25, 28, 32, 38, 40, 41, 44, 45, 47, 48, 50, 61
oval/egg-shaped 17, **17**, 24, **25**, 38, **39**, 40-41, 44, 50, 51, 62, 71
photos of **52**, 53, **53**
wreckage attributed to 27, 28, 29, **29**, 30, 31, **31**, 32, 33
UFO sightings 4, 6, 8, 15, 32, 43, 53, 54, 58, 69
in Central America 57
in the Dominican Republic 13-15
in Europe 12-13, 18-19, 38-41, **40**, 43-44, 47, 50-51, 67, 72
in New Guinea 19-21, **20**
in New Zealand 9-11, **10**
in North America 6-8, 8-9, 16, 21, 22-24, 26-33, 36-38, 41, 42-43, 44-45, 48-50, 51, 52, 54, 62
in South America 4-6, 15, 24-25, **25**, 45, 68
USAF (United States Air Force) 8, 27, 28, 31, 32, 33, 64, 77
USOs 13

Wanderka, Josef 50-51
Wartena, Udo 48-50
weather balloons **26**, 27, 28, 30, 31, 77
Weiner, Jim 69
Wilcox
Gary 50, 51
George 30, 32
Wilder, Leonard 65
Wilding, Marilyn 8
Wilmot, Mr. and Mrs. Dan 28
Wilson, Frieda 22
Wolski, Jan 60-61
Woody, William 28

Zamora, Lonnie 16-17, **16**